Fig. 2.

Porcelain

THE SMITHSONIAN ILLUSTRATED LIBRARY OF ANTIQUES

General Editor: Brenda Gilchrist

Porcelain

Jerry E. Patterson

COOPER-HEWITT MUSEUM

The Smithsonian Institution's National Museum of Design

ENDPAPERS

Scene in a porcelain factory: painters, muffle kiln, preparing the paste, repairers. Illustration from de Milly's *L'Art de la porcelaine*, 1771

FRONTISPIECE

Among eighteenth-century German porcelain factories was Fulda, which was in production between 1764 and 1790. The figures made there, now rare, are of very high quality. *The Immaculate Virgin on the Globe, Treading on a Serpent.* German, about 1780. Height: 37 cm. (14½ in.). Mark: *FF*, crowned, in underglaze blue. Cooper-Hewitt Museum, gift of the Trustees of the Estate of James Hazen Hyde

Art Direction, Design: JOSEPH B. DEL VALLE

Text Editor: JOAN HOFFMAN

Picture Editor: LISA LITTLE

Contents

Porcelain

1 Introduction

Porcelain collecting is a pursuit with a long and noble history and a busy and prosperous present. The special charms of porcelain have made it a collector's delight for centuries; few kinds of collecting have a grander pedigree. For more than a thousand years porcelain has been esteemed in China, where it was first made, and for five hundred years it has been cherished and collected in the West. Study and collecting began soon after the first translucent ceramics were made.

Today's collector begins against an impressive background. Fine porcelain has been enthusiastically collected in the Far East by royalty and mandarins, and in the West by such diverse figures as Madame de Pompadour, Frederick the Great, J. P. Morgan and Mark Twain. Centuries ago Chinese scholars were writing poetic praises of porcelain and establishing a hierarchy of taste among the various wares. Porcelain was eagerly received in Europe; from the first, Europeans found it irresistible.

Now porcelain is more widely appreciated and collected than ever before, and there are more types available. The beginning collector is encouraged to know that the supply, aside from inevitable rarities, is ample. Far from drying up, the stock increases constantly because fine porcelain is being made in many parts of the world. Surprisingly large amounts of antique porcelain, some of it very old, are in existence, often in the hands of private collectors and dealers from whom it eventually comes on the market. Trade in antique porcelain is vigorous, especially in Europe and Japan. International auctions from Hong Kong to Monte Carlo specialize in porcelains. Scientific aids for the identification and dating of porcelain are being developed. Scholarly publications helpful to the collector frequently appear. While fashions in porcelain collecting change—some wares were more popular fifty or even ten years ago than they are today—the enthusiasm persists.

Colorplate 1.
Meissen handleless cup (teabowl), with red-violet ground, and saucer, decorated with harbor scenes. German, about 1735–45. Height of cup: 4.3 cm. (1⅝ in.). Diameter of saucer: 11.8 cm. (4⅝ in.). Mark: crossed swords in underglaze blue. Cooper-Hewitt Museum, bequest of Erskine Hewitt

Porcelain is elegant and aristocratic; kings and emperors figure largely in its early history, and to this day, even when mass-produced as comparatively inexpensive tableware, porcelain maintains its prestige.

The attractions of porcelain as both useful ware and collector's item are easy to list. First and most noticeably, porcelain is smooth, white and translucent. (Translucency varies and can be difficult to detect but is present in all porcelain.) Porcelain is hard and can resist the cut of a steel knife, for example. Nonporous, porcelain is suitable for holding liquids of all kinds. Porcelain's smooth white surface seems to demand decoration. Its high tactility invites touch and makes it pleasant to handle. A certain glitter appeals to the eye. A malleable material, porcelain can be shaped into useful and pleasing forms. It lends itself to articles of style, luxury and charm.

Porcelain even has an engaging name, given to it, probably, by Marco Polo, who called it *porcellana*, the Italian word for the cowrie shell, which it resembles in color and texture.

Porcelain is resonant when struck. Few ears find the sound pleasant, but resonance is a good test to see if an object is actually porcelain (pottery clinks rather than rings when struck). Cracked pieces do not ring, and the ring of an inferior grade tends to be somewhat muffled.

The qualities of whiteness, hardness and translucency have always made porcelain more esteemed than earthenware. Sophisticated techniques, primarily because of the high kiln temperatures required, are necessary to produce porcelain; earthenware can be created by a single potter. Porcelain has always been more or less mass-produced; in the

Workmen in a Cantonese factory packing porcelain for shipment abroad. Chinese painting, probably late eighteenth century. British Museum, London

history of porcelain the names of modelers and designers often appear but seldom those of the actual potters.

There are three major categories of porcelain: hard-paste (*pâte dure*) porcelain, soft-paste (*pâte tendre*) porcelain and bone china. Each has its following of devoted students and collectors.

To make *hard-paste*, or *true*, *porcelain*—the terms are used interchangeably in this book—two special ingredients are required. The first is *china clay*, or *kaolin* (from Kao-ling, in China, where it was first found), a fine white clay that results from the decomposition by weathering of rocks containing feldspar (aluminum silicate). When kaolin is fired at a high temperature (above about 1350 degrees Celsius), a hard white material is produced. Relatively few parts of the world have deposits of kaolin. The scattered locations (China; Saxony, Germany; Cornwall, England) have influenced the course of porcelain history.

The second indispensable ingredient of hard-paste porcelain is *china stone*, also called *petuntse* (the French derivative of the Chinese name, *pai-tun-tzu*). Translucency is supplied by the addition of petuntse, a feldspathic stone, which is mined. Before use it has to be pulverized, washed and sieved, and, after being combined with kaolin, allowed to mature. Marco Polo and the very few other early Western travelers to China saw heaps of this mixture lying outdoors near the factories that produced porcelain and assumed that the mystery of the process (the Chinese refused then and later to reveal how porcelain was made) lay in the aging of the clay.

The matured mixture of kaolin and petuntse, referred to as the *paste* or *body*, is combined with water to make a plastic substance to

Transporting porcelain from Ching-te-chen to Canton over the Meiling Pass. Chinese painting, probably late eighteenth century. British Museum, London

be shaped either on a potter's wheel, in baked clay molds or by hand. The wheel is used to make such objects as pots, vases and plates; these wares the Chinese call *round wares*. The baked clay molds, filled with the plastic mass, are used to make figures. After firing, pieces made from several molds are assembled by using *slip*, clay that has been thinned with water. The workmen who do this assembling are traditionally known as *repairers*.

The shaped ware is put into a kiln and fired at a very high temperature, around 1300 or 1400 degrees Celsius. In the past, when firewood or coal was used to heat kilns, firing could take days. Today electric or gas kilns are used. Fired, the body becomes vitrified and impermeable. All sorts of things can go wrong during the firing. Forms can sag, shrink or collapse altogether. A series of fine cracks can develop (this is termed *crazing*), especially if the ware is withdrawn from the kiln too soon. Porcelain usually shrinks about ten percent in firing, which has to be allowed for. Only the heat should reach the porcelain: it is protected against the kiln's flames by being placed in a clay box called a *sagger*.

Porcelain that has been fired but not glazed is known as *biscuit* (or *bisque*). Resembling white marble, it has been used to imitate sculpture. But more often porcelain is glazed. *Glaze* is a thin coating of a glassy compound, generally lead or alkaline, often containing petuntse, which has the quality of fusing with the porcelain upon firing to form an extremely hard surface. Various colored glazes are produced by the oxides of different metals. A yellow glaze comes from adding a small quantity of antimony, violet from manganese, red and green from copper, and brown and green from iron. Innumerable shades are produced by varying the temperature and the amount of oxygen in the kiln. Glaze is applied to the object by immersion or spraying. In China the ware was shaped, dried, glazed and fired once. In Europe there is a different sequence: shaping, drying, firing (producing biscuit), then glazing and firing again.

Glaze that is *crackled* has a pattern of small cracks that originate in the firing, either by accident or intentionally for effect. The body of porcelain and the glaze have differing rates of expansion and contraction when subjected to heat or cold. Glaze, the applied and weaker part, cracks because of the tension set up by these differing rates. Although crackling does not have to take place during the firing, it usually does. In ancient times, by the year A.D. 1000 at least, Chinese potters came to understand crackle very well indeed, and many of the finest wares, especially in the Sung and Ch'ing periods, have crackle of great artistic merit (see colorplate 14). The Chinese were able to produce crackle in desired sizes and patterns and on various parts of individual pieces. For instance, some vessels have crackle that is smaller at the top of the vessel than at the bottom, and figures exist on which all parts have been crackled except the face and hands. The idea of the beauty of crackle is peculiarly Chinese, and, except for a relatively few connoisseurs in the West, only the Chinese have truly appreciated its refinements.

Painted decoration can be applied to the dried ware before glazing (underglaze decoration), in which case firing is required to fix it. Only such colors as cobalt blue and copper red, which can withstand the high glaze temperatures, can be employed. Underglaze decoration cannot be felt on the piece. Painted decoration in *enamels* is applied over the glaze; this overglaze decoration can be felt by running the hands over the object because the enamels are fired on at a lower temperature and do not sink into the glaze. Signs of wear may become evident. The palette for overglaze decoration includes a wide range of colors.

Soft-paste, or *artificial, porcelain* is traditionally associated with the early French factories although it has been made in many countries. The most famous soft-paste porcelain is eighteenth-century Sèvres. Most eighteenth-century English porcelain is also soft-paste. Since the early years of the nineteenth century, however, soft-paste porcelain has rarely been used, and little, if any, is made today.

Not readily distinguishable by the eye from hard-paste, soft-paste shows a granular surface where chipped, whereas true porcelain is flintlike in cross section. Also, the glaze does not appear to be one with the body as in true porcelain. Over the centuries, generations of collectors have found soft-paste porcelain warmer in feel than true porcelain.

The manufacturing process of soft-paste was always time-consuming and expensive. Petuntse and kaolin were not used. Sand, alum, sea salt, gypsum, soda and nitrate were combined into a glassy mixture called *frit* and melted. The recipe varied from factory to factory but usually included these ingredients. Soapstone was sometimes added. The frit was pounded into a powder and mixed with white clay and water, then dried, crushed and sifted, and mixed again with water to form the paste. Once modeled, it was fired at about 1000 degrees Celsius, or higher, producing a biscuit, which was sprayed with a lead oxide glaze. After another firing at less than 1000 degrees Celsius, overglaze decoration was applied, which required a further firing to fix the enamel colors. If *gilding* was used in decoration, and many French and English soft-paste porcelains were gilded, yet another, final firing was needed. Kiln losses from these firings were heavy. The soft-paste was inclined to craze. The ware often had to be propped up on wooden pegs, and these left rough places on the *foot* of the porcelain that had to be ground off on a wheel before the piece was ready for sale. Nevertheless, this tedious process resulted in superb porcelain with decoration so fused with the glaze that they seem of a piece.

As a useful substance, soft-paste certainly has drawbacks: it chips easily, stains, shows scratches, and cracks in very hot water. It was always much better suited for cabinet articles than for tablewares yet many services were made at French and English soft-paste factories. The extreme beauty of the material and its ability to take decoration so smoothly compensated for its fragility.

The third major category of porcelain is *bone china*, which has been the standard English porcelain since the early nineteenth century. The ash of burned animal bones is added to a basic hard-paste of kaolin and petuntse. This bone ash can at times make up as much as half the body. Historically, the use of bone ash in English porcelain is traced to the middle of the eighteenth century, but stabilization of the mix into the formula, credited to Josiah Spode II, that has become world-famous as English bone china did not occur until about 1800. The material is easily handled since it is less prone to collapse in the kiln than the glassy frit. It is more durable than most porcelain and takes both transfer-printed and painted decoration.

Transfer-printed decoration, another English invention of the mid-eighteenth century, was a process whereby an engraved picture was transferred to the surface of china, either over or under the glaze (see plates 64, 65 and 67). An engraved copperplate was inked and the design put onto paper. While it was still wet, the design was pressed onto the porcelain, leaving an imprint. During the eighteenth century black, blue, purple and red printing was used; other colors were added later. Transfer-printed decoration spread to the Continent early in the nineteenth century but was never as extensively used there as it was in England. Another difference is that on the Continent it was first used on earthenware, then porcelain; in England it was the other way around.

A word must be said about the marks of origin and identification found on porcelain. Such marks can be of value to the collector, but they can also be misleading. On the whole, most experts today believe that in establishing the origin and value of a piece of porcelain marks are secondary to style and quality. It must be emphasized that many pieces of porcelain, including some of the greatest value—from all periods and all factories—are unmarked. The extreme irregularity of systems of marks must also be underscored. In the past the mark was not regarded as an immutable thing: a single factory might employ literally dozens of marks over quite a short period of manufactory, and the same mark might well be drawn in several ways. Lack of uniformity in drawing and spelling is commonplace. In addition to the factory mark, marks of various kinds were made by modelers, deco-

rators and other craftsmen, and dealers. Few, if any, porcelain factories have had an absolutely regular system of marks; therefore, the
collector must not be misled into thinking that the absence of a mark
or an irregularity in a mark necessarily detracts from the value of the
piece. Marks have also been tampered with, especially during the
nineteenth century, when collectors tended to stress their importance.

All that noted, many collectors still find the study of marks a
valuable and challenging exercise in research and study and an aid to
identification of examples. Many works, some of enormous length with
thousands of examples, have been compiled on Oriental and European
marks on porcelain; several of these are listed in the bibliography.

As far as the treatment of marks in the text is concerned, no attempt has been made to include descriptions of all the marks associated
with the various factories discussed. This would have been impossible.
Characteristic marks, or those most often used, are generally mentioned (some are also illustrated in the margin), but they are by no
means the only marks that might be found on porcelain from the factory in question. In the captions for the plates, of course, the marks are
given exactly as they appear on the pieces shown in the photographs.

The two main strands of porcelain making are the Far Eastern
and the European. Each has its distinctive history, yet the strands
have repeatedly crossed. The plan of this book is to trace these strands
in chronological order and to show where and how they have crossed
and in what ways they have influenced each other.

2　Early Porcelain of the Far East

The study of Chinese porcelain, like that of other Chinese art, is organized along historical lines based on dynastic periods such as T'ang, Ming, Ch'ing. Each piece of porcelain is usually identified first by dynasty, to fix it in time, then by type of ware. The classification is not uniform: some Chinese porcelains, especially those of the eighteenth century, are more likely to be referred to by the name of the ruler in whose reign they were made than by dynastic name, for example, K'ang-hsi (emperor, 1662–1722) rather than Ch'ing. The dynasties that most concern the porcelain collector are:

T'ang	618–906
Sung	960–1279
Northern Sung	960–1127
Southern Sung	1127–1279
Yüan	1280–1368
Ming	1368–1644
Ch'ing	1644–1912

The first true porcelain was made, it is generally believed, under the T'ang dynasty, but the period is much better known to collectors for its pottery.

Under the Sung dynasty the finest porcelains in history, in the opinion of many students, were produced by hundreds of kilns in both northern and southern China. The imperial ware (*kuan yao*), which was specially made for the court of the emperor, is today considered a summit not only of porcelain art but of all Chinese art. Most Sung porcelain is of extremely high quality, with outstanding monochrome glazes.

Among the best-known Sung wares is *ying ch'ing*, which has a glaze tinged with very pale shadowy blue. Like many porcelains, it varies a great deal in quality. Decoration, incised or molded, is understated, with floral designs, fish, ducks or human figures as motifs.

Sung Dynasty 960–1279

Vase

Flower dish

Bulb bowl

Colorplate 2.
Lung-ch'üan stoneware in the famous celadon glaze, a mallet-shaped vase (*kinuta*) with pair of fish handles. Chinese, Southern Sung, twelfth century. Height: 25.9 cm. (10¼ in.). Unmarked. Freer Gallery of Art

The haunting color called celadon, which varies from delicate green to gray-blue, is famous in ceramic history. Objects glazed in that color are referred to as celadon. One type of Sung porcellanous stoneware glazed in this color is called Lung-ch'üan, after the district where it was made (colorplate 2). It was either undecorated or ornamented with molded or applied relief designs. When the reliefs, such as pairs of fish or panels with human figures, were left uncovered by glaze they turned red in the kiln, producing a most striking contrast with the overall gray. Celadon was made at a number of kilns over a long stretch of Chinese history. After Europe learned the art of porcelain making, this much-admired glaze was used at many European factories, too.

Another celebrated Sung ware sought by collectors today is Ting (plate 1). The white porcelain is covered with an ivory-colored glaze that imparts an orange translucency to the body. Decoration, largely floral, is carved or incised; the design is occasionally impressed. The creamy glaze is sometimes omitted from the mouth rims of the vessels; the rims are then bound with bands of silver or copper.

In view of the high prices Sung porcelain now commands, it is rather alarming to collectors to learn that as far back as the sixteenth century there were potters already renowned for their imitations of it.

These early porcelains have been treasured and displayed as objects of art in museums and private collections for so long that their original purpose, other than aesthetic, has become obscure. A real effort is required to look at one of these magnificent monochromes and remember that it was made for use. Sung porcelains included such useful objects as plates, bowls, incense burners, bulb pots, vases, ewers.

Roughly contemporary with the Sung in China was the Koryo period in Korea (918–1400). Superb celadons were made in Korea, where, in about 1100, there reportedly were eighteen porcelain-making centers with 150 kilns. Korean ceramics of this period, typically decorated under the glaze with cranes, waterfowls and willow trees, have long been collected in the West.

The Sung dynasty ended in 1279 with the fall of the Southern Sung Empire to the Mongol conquerors of the rest of China. The Mongol dynasty (Yüan) lasted from 1280 to 1368. Kublai Khan (1216–1294), founder of the line, is the Yüan ruler most familiar to Westerners. During his reign, Marco Polo visited the empire of China, an insignificant event so far as the Chinese were concerned but of enormous importance in the cultural history of Europe. Traditional porcelains continued to be made with few changes during the Yüan period. One noteworthy development was the use of underglaze painting in decoration, the most important underglaze color being the blue derived from cobalt (plate 2). This led to China's famous blue-and-white decoration.

1.
Ting ware bottle-shaped vase decorated in brown slip with peony scrolls, details incised. Chinese, Sung dynasty (960–1279). Height: 16.3 cm. (6½ in.). Unmarked. Freer Gallery of Art

2.
Cobalt blue, used on this large dish, was introduced into China in the early fourteenth century. The base of the dish is unglazed and has turned orange in the firing. Chinese, Yüan dynasty, fourteenth century. Diameter: 45.4 cm. (17⅞ in.). Unmarked. Freer Gallery of Art

3   4

3.
Large-mouthed jar of the *fa-hua* type painted with turquoise, aubergine, white, yellow and other enamels within slip outline. The *fa-hua* type, designed to simulate cloisonné enamel, is a perennial favorite of collectors in the West and has frequently been copied. Chinese, Ming dynasty, about 1500. Height: 30.5 cm. (12 in.). Unmarked. Freer Gallery of Art

4.
Jar with green and yellow overglaze enamel decoration of dragon and clouds with incised lines separating the two colors. Chinese, Ming dynasty, Chêng-te period (1506–21). Height: 11.3 cm. (4½ in.). Mark: four-character reign mark of Chêng-te. Freer Gallery of Art

The word "Ming," the name of the next dynasty (1368–1644), when applied to porcelain, is a term of high commendation. It is also a dangerous word that is used all too lightly by dealers and collectors. Because of the extreme enthusiasm, not to say reverence, with which Ming porcelain (plate 4) is regarded by collectors, there is a natural tendency to label many pieces as dating from this period. Ming types, especially those with painted decoration, persisted in subsequent centuries. The presence of certain forms and designs first evolved under the Ming dynasty does not necessarily mean the piece is of the period. Ming wares were also the first Chinese porcelains introduced into Europe in quantity and are therefore the most widely familiar.

The traditional glory of Ming porcelain is the polychrome painting with enamels on glazed porcelain (plate 3). The Ming painters had a rich palette; few porcelains have ever been more colorful. In "three-color" decoration (*san-ts'ai*), the colors were blue, turquoise, mauve, yellow and white (not actually three) used as washes, and in "five-color" painting (*wu-ts'ai*), turquoise, red, brown, yellow and gold. Typical subjects are flowers (lotus, peony [plate 5]), birds (cranes, peacocks), dragons and human figures.

Painting under the glaze also flourished in the Ming period, blue and red being the most usual colors, blue always the more popular. Blue-and-white decoration on Chinese ceramics seems to have been inspired by Islamic wares; one shade is called Mohammedan blue.

Ming Dynasty 1368–1644

Bottle

Stem cup

Bowl

5.
Among the Ming techniques of porcelain decoration is *tou-ts'ai,* "contrasting
colors," shown in this tiny stem cup with
underglaze blue and overglaze enamel
decoration. Chinese, Ming dynasty,
Chêng-hua period (1465–87). Height:
8 cm. (3⅛ in.). Mark: six-character reign
mark of Chêng-hua. Freer Gallery of Art

6

7

6.
Blanc de chine figure of the goddess Kuan Yin with child. Chinese, Ch'ing dynasty, K'ang-hsi period (1662–1722). Height: 30 cm. (11¾ in.). Unmarked. Cooper-Hewitt Museum

7.
Porcelain bowl with underglaze blue decoration, the outside view showing figures in a landscape with a pine. The decoration inside the bowl consists of a pine, a bamboo and a plum blossom, "the three friends of winter." Connoisseurs consider this the finest type of blue-and-white porcelain, with an unblemished, lustrous glaze. Chinese, Ming dynasty, second half of the fifteenth century. Diameter: 20.3 cm. (8 in.). Unmarked. Freer Gallery of Art

The painting, masterly and vigorous, has some echoes of the noble Chinese art of calligraphy. The objects on which this painting was lavished include flowerpots, incense burners, vases, bowls (plate 7), platters, covered temple jars, wine pots and barrel-shaped garden seats. Many Ming pieces, fishbowls and temple jars, for example, are of large size, the height of the jars four feet or more.

A porcelain with a fine-grained body covered with a thick white glaze but no painted decoration was first made at Tê-hua in Fukien province in the late Ming period. In the West it was given the name *blanc de chine*. Of special interest are the figures, often Taoist or Buddhist gods and saints, which continued to be made throughout the centuries (plate 6). Collectors in the West were so entranced by this porcelain that when porcelain making began in Europe *blanc de chine* was copied at many factories, including Sèvres in France and Chelsea in England.

3　Oriental Porcelain in Europe

few pieces of porcelain found their way into Europe during the Middle Ages. A Venetian museum has a white jar said to have been brought back from China by Marco Polo. Legends aside, it is clear that by the fifteenth century sufficient porcelain had reached Europe for artists to be conscious enough of its pictorial value to depict it in painting: the Italian artist Mantegna's *Adoration of the Magi*, painted about 1490, is the earliest-known European painting to show a piece of porcelain, a blue-and-white cup. Monarchs were able to add some pieces of porcelain to their jewelhouses and treasuries. Inventories show that Emperor Charles V, King Henry VIII and Queen Elizabeth I all owned porcelain.

Most of these pieces, which were usually cups or other hollow vessels, were mounted in silver, bronze or some other metal. The technique is known as monture and is used essentially to provide a frame or setting, much as is done in setting a jewel. The mounting for a vessel often consisted of a stand, a rim and a handle. Probably these mounts were meant originally to enhance as well as protect the fragile and valuable piece brought at great hazard from a faraway country. But the metal mount often transformed the purpose of the vessel: a Chinese vase supplied with a mount carrying a spout, for example, became a ewer. The earliest English example of a mounted Chinese bowl (a Sung dynasty piece) has a mount dated 1569. The English, and most other Europeans, were soon able to cure themselves of this custom, but not the French (see plate 42). They continued to embellish the porcelain that came their way from the Far East, and after porcelain was made in Europe they set to work on that, surrounding it with ormolu (gilded bronze).

The well-known xenophobia of the Chinese guaranteed that Europeans would have a difficult time entering the country, much less trading there. China had merchants, too, however, and despite the imperial government's reluctance to permit foreigners in the coun-

Scholars generally agree that the earliest appearance of Oriental porcelain in European painting occurs in Andrea Mantegna's *Adoration of the Magi*, part of a triptych painted about 1490. Bellini and Dürer also made early depictions of Oriental porcelain. Uffizi Gallery, Florence

8.
Medici porcelain plate depicting the death of King Saul. Italian, sixteenth century. Diameter: 33.3 cm. (13⅛ in.). Mark: coronet and six balls of the Medici arms. Metropolitan Museum of Art, Samuel D. Lee Fund, 1941

try, from about the middle of the sixteenth century some trade in porcelain and other products was carried on with the daring and persistent Portuguese, who managed to establish a settlement at Macao in 1557. From Macao, though carefully regulated, not to say harassed, by Chinese officialdom, they were allowed to visit Canton twice a year to acquire trade goods.

While in general the Chinese did not want European interlopers to learn much about China, in particular they did not want them to learn the method of making porcelain. The very mystery is an indication of the esteem in which porcelain was held. The Chinese were successful in preserving the secrecy of their process until the middle of the nineteenth century, long after Europeans had made porcelain on their own. Few trade secrets have such a long history.

Porcelain was imported from China only with long delays and at great expense. There were many hazards between the Far East and Europe—shipwreck, robbers by land and sea, warfare. Clearly, the best thing would be to make one's own porcelain at home. This was much easier said than done.

When the Europeans first tried their hands at porcelain what resulted was very much an imitation of the Chinese, and a pretty poor one at that. One famous attempt was the Medici porcelain made in Florence under the aegis of Francesco Maria de' Medici, Grand Duke of Tuscany, around 1575 (plate 8). This porcelain, which is soft-paste, is not very pretty, often misshapen, and has a grayish glaze. Historians have paid great attention to Medici porcelain because it was the first made in Europe. For most of today's collectors, however, interest can only be historical: a mere sixty-one pieces are recorded, and fourteen of those have been missing since the nineteenth century! The chances of new pieces turning up are minute, but it has happened, and recently. A small bowl (completely blue-and-white Chinese in shape and decoration) was found in 1973 at Elizabeth Seton College in Yonkers, New York, where it was being used as a sugar bowl. It caused a sensation when it was sold for the largest amount ever brought by a European ceramic.

Medici porcelain and a few French attempts were not good enough, and Europeans continued to import Oriental porcelain. The Portuguese held absolute sway over the Eastern trade until the beginning of the seventeenth century, when the Dutch, first as pirates hijacking Portuguese ships, then as legitimate traders, began to establish themselves in the Far East. In 1602, they formed their celebrated Dutch East India Company. Its ships got to the island of Formosa in 1624, and for nearly twenty years the Dutch ran a trading settlement there for goods coming from China. In 1638, they established a monopoly on trade with Japan, which had an important effect, as will be shown, on the history of porcelain. In 1699, the English finally got a ship into Canton, but the average European was still indebted to the Dutch for his porcelain.

Every new collector must wonder about the quantity of old Chinese porcelain that is available for purchase. How can there be so much of the genuine article around? The answer is that unimaginable amounts of Chinese porcelain were brought into Europe in the seventeenth and eighteenth centuries. Records exist of single ships carrying 100,000 pieces. Historians have estimated that between 1602 and 1657 more than 3,000,000 pieces of Chinese porcelain were shipped into Europe in Dutch ships. Between 1659 and 1682 more than 190,000 pieces of Japanese porcelain were imported.

The Dutch were responsible not only for bringing Japanese porcelain into Europe but for its creation in the first place. Japan has a formidably ancient tradition of pottery making that goes back to prehistoric times. The Dutch were not interested in pottery, however, and the Japanese, eager to trade, soon began to turn out porcelains based on Chinese and Korean models to satisfy European tastes. They themselves continued to prefer their pottery to their porcelain.

9.
Oval-shaped bowl decorated in the Kakiemon style with a design of plum blossom, pine and rocks of characteristic simplicity. Japanese, Edo period (1615–1868). Length: 40.7 cm. (16 in.). Unmarked. Freer Gallery of Art

Colorplate 3.
Kutani ware large porcelain dish. The inner surface of the dish has hexagonal shapes in a design called tortoise shell. Birds and flower motifs within the hexagons alternate with purely abstract shapes. The outer surface is decorated in underglaze blue. Japanese, Edo period, seventeenth century. Diameter: 33.6 cm. (13¼ in.). Unmarked. Freer Gallery of Art

Kaolin was discovered in Japan at Arita, around 1616, and the first Japanese porcelain kilns were built there soon afterward. The earliest decoration in polychrome enamels is very much associated with the celebrated family of Japanese potters of whom the most famous representative is the mid-seventeenth-century Sakaida Kakiemon. He gave his name to an elegant, restrained, asymmetrical style of overglaze painting in red, yellow, green and blue enamels with delicate flowers, pine trees, birds, and the tiger, dragon and phoenix, among other motifs. This beautiful Kakiemon style of painting (plate 9) made a great impression on Europeans and was copied and imitated at Meissen, Chantilly (see plate 38), Chelsea (see plate 53), Bow and Worcester.

Another type of ware, known as Imari, was produced at Arita and exported from the late seventeenth century on. Typical of Imari wares, except for the earliest period, when underglaze blue alone was used, was strong blue, red and gold painting almost totally covering the surface. The style, much imitated in the West, especially by the nineteenth-century English factories, has endured into the twentieth century.

At Kutani, in the late seventeenth century, striking and diverse porcelain was made, decorated in enamels of a wide variety of color and design (colorplate 3). The manufacture of Kutani ware lapsed toward the end of the seventeenth century but was revived in the nineteenth by the Yoshidaya family. Among the most sought-after Kutani wares from that period are those decorated in gold on a coral red ground.

Other Japanese porcelains collected today in both Japan and the West are Nabeshima (made after 1675), decorated in underglaze blue and enamels, and Hirado (made from 1712), also with underglaze blue decoration—often including figures of children—or relief decoration.

Generally speaking, Oriental porcelains sent to Europe before the late seventeenth century were products made and decorated in the prevailing native taste of China, Japan or Korea. Although large amounts were exported to Europe, for the most part the wares were not made or decorated especially for that purpose. Beginning in the late seventeenth century, however, much Oriental porcelain was expressly made for export to the West, sometimes to the Western taste and decoration. This porcelain, which is primarily an eighteenth-century phenomenon, is mostly known as Chinese export porcelain or China trade porcelain (or Japanese export porcelain, etc.). It is not always easy to distinguish between porcelain in the Oriental taste, which of course also continued to be sent to the West, and export porcelain. (See Chapter 8 for a discussion of Chinese export porcelain.)

Because of the tremendous importations from China and Japan, the average well-to-do European could have his pick of Eastern porcelain from the seventeenth century on. As might be expected, European economists of the day began to complain that too much money was leaving their countries to buy this attractive foreign merchandise. In England Daniel Defoe said that "chinamania" was ruining whole families, and an anguished Saxon minister of finance cried that "China is the bleeding bowl of Saxony." Efforts to make porcelain in Europe were redoubled.

Two Oriental potters throw vessels on wheels while other workmen knead clay. Picture Collection, Cooper-Hewitt Museum Library

4 The First European Porcelain

No European prince who collected Oriental porcelain in the early years of the eighteenth century treasured his vases and bowls more than Augustus II, Elector of Saxony and King of Poland, called "the Strong." Augustus (1670–1733) is remembered more for his pursuit of porcelain and his successful sponsorship of the first true European porcelain than for his physical strength, awesome love life, or spectacular conversion from Lutheranism to Catholicism to gain the throne of Poland. He was the greatest collector of porcelain in European history, the patron saint, as it were, of china collecting.

Augustus, from the beginning of his reign, bought Chinese and Japanese porcelain in massive quantities; his ministers and subjects were appalled at the expenditure. But the king wanted to be more than Europe's major collector of imported china. He wanted to have porcelain made right in his domains; he was determined to have his own factory.

More than a century had gone by since the brief manufacture of Medici porcelain. Louis Poterat had made soft-paste at Rouen, France, during the last quarter of the seventeenth century, but the factory was never successful and only a few examples of its work are known. The one other factory was that at St. Cloud, near Paris, which also produced soft-paste porcelain in small amounts. Oddly enough, after Europeans had been trying for more than a hundred years without notable success to make porcelain, when Augustus decided he must have his own factory, everything suddenly fell into place. The first European true or hard-paste porcelain was produced in Saxony just five years after the initial experiments.

An accomplished and scientifically minded Bohemian nobleman, Ehrenfried Walter, Count von Tschirnhaus, had already been experimenting with methods of obtaining very high temperatures, usually from solar energy. Such high temperatures were indispensable to the

Colorplate 4.
Before Johann Böttger made the first true
European porcelain at Meissen, he produced a red stoneware there that has
been given his name. The surface of
Böttger's stoneware lent itself to polish-
ing, producing an elegant effect, often
further enriched, as in this case, with
engraving. Interlaced initials are engraved in a framework of scrolls under
a crown. The mounting is gilded brass.
German, about 1715. Height: 21.4 cm.
(8⅜ in.). Unmarked. Cooper-Hewitt
Museum, purchased in memory of Mrs.
John Innes Kane

Colorplate 5.
Chinoiserie decoration enlivens this Meissen lantern-shaped clock case attributed
to Johann Gottlob Kirchner. The decoration is in the style of Johann Gregor
Herold. The figures peeping around the
sides are satyrs; a cat sits on top. German, about 1730–32. Height: 42.3 cm.
(16⅝ in.). Mark: crossed swords in
underglaze blue. Cooper-Hewitt Museum, gift of Irwin Untermyer

manufacture of true porcelain. In 1703, Augustus added to Tschirnhaus's endeavors the services of another expert, Johann Friedrich
Böttger, who is generally credited with the invention of true porcelain
on the European continent.

Böttger had the reputation of being something of a rogue. He
had been working as alchemist to the king of Prussia, attempting to
transmute lead into gold. He had naturally failed in that endeavor and
was rapidly finding Prussia too hot for comfort, having spent a great
deal of the king's money without result. Nevertheless, Augustus the
Strong, desperately looking for gold to pay for his Polish campaigns
and the most sumptuous court in Europe, hired him as alchemist.

Böttger failed again of course and was soon assigned to Tschirnhaus as assistant. Not at all anxious to be put to work trying to make
porcelain, he appears to have believed it impossible at first. In those
days, however, there was no arguing with a king, so Böttger reluc-
tantly went to work in the laboratory supplied by Augustus (colorplate 4). He was disgruntled enough to write on his own front door:
"A goldmaker has been turned into a potmaker." In fact, he attempted
to run away two or three times only to be dragged back when caught
by Augustus's soldiers and imprisoned in disgrace.

The date of birth of true European porcelain is known from
Böttger's kiln records, which show that on January 15, 1708, after
a twelve-hour firing, he achieved a white, translucent body. Kaolin
had been found at Colditz, alabaster was used in place of petuntse,
and Tschirnhaus's experiments had supplied the required heat.

Augustus was delighted with the samples of porcelain sent to
him. His ministers were understandably less enthusiastic, foreseeing
still more expenditure on useless breakables. Furthermore, they de-
tested Böttger, who drank, was quarrelsome and generally unpopular.
In spite of ministerial reluctance, Augustus decreed into existence
the Royal Saxon Porcelain Manufactory on January 23, 1710. Head-
quarters were in the Albrechtsburg in Meissen, the very fortress
where, five years earlier, Böttger had been imprisoned when he was
caught running away from his laboratory.

Meissen, the site of the creation of true European porcelain and
its first manufactory, is a suburb of the city of Dresden, in the region
then called Saxony, which is now part of East Germany. The factory
is still in operation. The porcelain made there has been persistently and
incorrectly called Dresden by English-speaking people. That name
is used today by collectors to denote some copies of original Meissen,
especially figures, made in the nineteenth and twentieth centuries.
The French have always called Meissen *porcelaine de Saxe*.

Once Böttger had succeeded with the porcelain body, the next
steps were to model and paint the ware to the standard of Oriental
imports. Böttger told Augustus that his porcelain was "as good as the
East India Company porcelain." This was true of the body because

COLORPLATE 4

COLORPLATE 5

10.
Early Meissen teapot with painted decoration and gilding probably by Bar-
tolomäus Seuter of Augsburg, a well-
known *Hausmaler*. German, about 1730–
35. Height: 12.1 cm. (4¾ in.). Mark:
rust-red cross. Metropolitan Museum of
Art, gift of R. Thornton Wilson, 1950,
in memory of Florence Ellsworth Wilson

the materials used at Meissen were equal to those in China, but the
painted decoration was inferior to its Chinese models, at least at first.
Within a few years a series of master potters and painters changed
that and brought Meissen to a high level of technical and artistic
skill (plate 10).

Meissen had master modelers whose names are known and whose
style makes their work identifiable even though it is not signed. The
conclusions as to authorship made from sight and feel are a major
part of porcelain connoisseurship.

Böttger was the first modeler. His career after his great discovery
was, however, short. He could never organize the Meissen factory
properly, and it limped along under his direction. At the time of his
death in 1719—not surprisingly from alcoholism—there were only
twenty-four workmen at Meissen. But great days were in the offing.

Johann Gottlob Kirchner joined Meissen as modeler in 1727 and
was there off and on until 1733 (colorplate 5); he was dismissed more
than once for "unseemly conduct" or "inefficiency." At other times
he was rather engagingly described as "frivolous." Augustus put
Kirchner, and indeed the entire Meissen staff, to work on porcelain for
one of the most bizarre projects in the history of taste—the Japanese
Palace. This was a large mansion in Dresden that was to be furnished
and, literally, filled with porcelain. Various rooms were reserved, each
with a different color scheme, for Chinese, Japanese and Meissen
wares. Before Augustus died in 1733, the number of pieces imported
or made for the palace amounted to no fewer than 35,798.

Augustus, who had no understanding of the limitations of the
material, wanted big pieces of porcelain. He was disappointed that

Böttger could not produce enormous vases in the Chinese style. For the Japanese Palace he ordered Kirchner and the other workmen to model numerous domestic and wild animals—life-size. Kirchner managed to make, among others, a lion, a pelican and a lynx. Some of these curiosities still exist.

Kirchner worked—and quarreled—with the best-known Meissen modeler, one of the most celebrated names in porcelain, Johann Joachim Kändler. Kändler came to the factory in 1731, and stayed forty years. Ranked as *Modellmeister*, he was probably the highest-paid worker in the factory. At times he had a hundred workmen under his direction. These workmen made molds from the figures modeled by the Meissen sculptors, who did not shape each figure individually. Among Kändler's assistants, two who gained individual fame as modelers were Johann Friedrich Eberlein and Peter Reinicke (plate 11). Figures by all these men are much sought by collectors today.

11.
Meissen figure of Asia from the Four Continents, a popular set. The original model of about 1745 is attributed to Peter Reinicke; this example was made later in the eighteenth century, or possibly in the nineteenth. Height: 30.5 cm. (12 in.). Unmarked. Cooper-Hewitt Museum, gift of the Trustees of the Estate of James Hazen Hyde

The monkey motif enchanted eighteenth-century Europeans, and *singeries* depicting monkeys were found everywhere. Three monkey musicians, for example, enliven this embroidered waistcoat pocket. French, late eighteenth century. Cooper-Hewitt Museum, bequest of Richard Cranch Greenleaf, in memory of his mother, Adeline Emma Greenleaf

Colorplate 6.
Long-haired Bolognese hounds were modeled at Meissen more than once by Johann Gottlob Kirchner, including at least one for Augustus the Strong's Japanese Palace. German, about 1733. Height: 42.6 cm. (16¾ in.). Unmarked. Metropolitan Museum of Art, gift of R. Thornton Wilson, 1954, in memory of Florence Ellsworth Wilson

Kändler probably created—estimates vary—more than a thousand different figures and figure groups. They have been endlessly reproduced, copied and pirated, but the originals are unsurpassed in charm and in skill of design. Among the extraordinary wealth of Kändler's work, it is difficult to say what he did best. His birds and animals are much admired. What keen observation they reveal, and how wide their variety—squirrels, pugs (plate 12), swans, parrots, monkeys, terriers. Augustus was a great huntsman, and for him Kändler did a series of wild animals—wolves, stags, boar, bears—being brought down by sporting dogs.

On another level of animal sculpture, Kändler and his assistants created the celebrated *Affenkapelle*, or "monkey band" (actually an orchestra), a set of twenty-one monkey musician figures with a conductor. The story goes—it is the kind of art object that requires a story—that this group is a satire on a court orchestra that Kändler disliked. The story is pat but probably not true: *singeries*, representations of monkeys in human garb or engaged in human activities, were highly fashionable motifs at the time. Nineteenth-century collectors adored the monkey band: many strove for years to complete a set. The figures were constantly reproduced and copied, not only at Meissen but at Vienna, Derby, Chelsea and other factories. Twentieth-century taste finds them less interesting than the Kändler animals depicted in their natural state and observed with a scientific eye. Many of these have distinct personalities that make them captivating. They are also generally less stylized than Kirchner's animal figures (colorplate 6). Both sculptors worked from the animals in Augustus's private zoo.

The eighteenth century thought in terms of sets; much of Kändler's work, and that of the other artisans, was in sets: Four Seasons, Four Elements, Four Continents (see plate 11), Tradesmen, Dancers and Italian Comedy figures, for example. The sets made a brave show when displayed on mantelpiece and sideboard.

Meissen crinoline figures, made by Kändler and other master modelers, are ladies in immense spreading skirts, often holding a lapdog, receiving the attentions of a cavalier obliged to keep his distance by the billowing dress. Crinoline figures apparently seem fussy to collectors now; their great era of popularity was the Victorian Age.

Among other Meissen figures, the dwarfs, hunchbacks and other deformed figures made after engravings by the French artist Jacques Callot, who had been dead a century, are especially notable. Callot figures were made later at the Vienna, Cozzi (see plate 32), Chelsea and Derby factories. To modern eyes dwarfs and hunchbacks are not humorous subjects, but in the eighteenth century they were thought hilarious, and the figures were very popular.

The celebrated figures were only part of the Meissen production. Heinrich, Count von Brühl, chief minister of Saxony, became

12.
Pug dogs (*Möpser*) were fashionable pets at the Saxon court. This Meissen brown-spotted pug by Johann Joachim Kändler wears a collar dated 1741. Height: 22.3 cm. (8¾ in.). Mark: crossed swords in blue. Cooper-Hewitt Museum, purchased in memory of Mrs. John Innes Kane

director of the factory in 1733, and from then until the Seven Years' War began in 1756 Meissen enjoyed its most splendid period. Magnificent tablewares were manufactured during the Brühl regime. The European invention of porcelain coincided with an era of great elegance in everything to do with the consumption of food and drink. Eating in sixteenth-century Europe was not far removed from medieval slovenliness. Royalty and the high nobility were presented with their goblets and dishes by kneeling attendants, but higgledy-piggledy was good enough for everybody else. The wooden trencher was still held in the lap and the spoon and a piece of bread sufficed for implements. The seventeenth and eighteenth centuries, especially the latter, changed that, at least for the well-to-do, and a vast amount of new tableware was required for the proper serving of meals. Much of this was fine porcelain, although silver never lost its place on the table.

Meals on state occasions lasted for a long time and were divided into many more courses than they are today, concluding after several hours with tea and coffee. The table was handsomely arranged and decorated. The dessert in particular was the focus of great aesthetic effort. For important events it was prepared on another table, and guests were invited to walk around and admire it before consuming it. Centerpieces, some extremely large, were created in porcelain for the table. A Greek temple, together with a crowd of as many as forty small classical figures, was characteristic. Sometimes an entire porcelain village was set up, complete with human figures and livestock. The candlesticks and wall sconces that illuminated the scene were often of porcelain, too. Many of the individual figures now found in antique shops were once components of these decorations.

Porcelain tablewares consisted of plates, covered dishes, tureens, tankards, platters, sweetmeat dishes and mustard pots, among many other forms. Some of the service pieces, especially tureens, were in lifelike shapes of vegetables and animals. Forks, which by the middle of the seventeenth century were in fairly common use, and knives frequently had porcelain handles (plate 13). Even skillets and tea kettles were of porcelain.

Utensils for the three great warm drinks—tea, coffee and chocolate—accounted for a considerable percentage of Meissen's production (plate 14) and would become staples of later European porcelain factories, too. Chocolate, New World in origin, was introduced to Europe by the Spaniards. Europeans were not very quick at taking it up. It was drunk hot but undiluted and unsweetened. Not until the early eighteenth century did the English think to add milk, whereupon the drink became widely popular in aristocratic circles. Too expensive for the common herd, chocolate was a favored drink of royalty. Consequently the pots, cups and saucers designed for chocolate drinking tend to be of noticeably high quality and elegantly painted.

13.
Knife and fork with Meissen porcelain handles and Augsburg metalwork. German, about 1740. Length of knife: 23.1 cm. (9⅛ in.). Length of fork: 18.5 cm. (7¼ in.). Marks, on the metalwork: ellipse containing the letter C, inverted bunch of grapes, oval with a lion rampant. Cooper-Hewitt Museum, gift of the Misses Hewitt

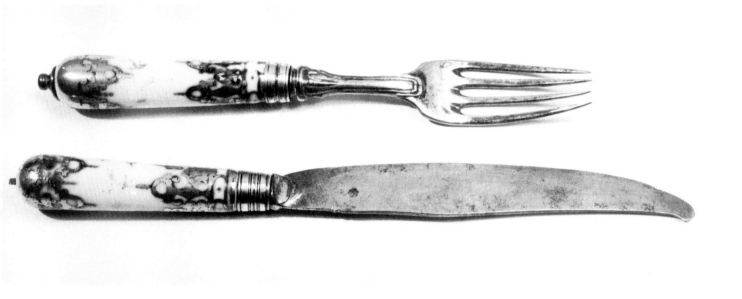

14.
Among the many special drinking vessels made at Meissen was the *trembleuse* cup and saucer with a raised well-ring holding the cup in place, designed for invalids' use. German, 1763–74. Height: 5.5 cm. (2⅛ in.). Mark: crossed swords in underglaze blue. Cooper-Hewitt Museum, bequest of Georgiana L. McClellan

Tea and coffee were introduced into Europe early in the seventeenth century and became popular beverages by the century's end. At first frightening rumors circulated about the dangers of drinking them. Pregnant women who drank coffee were said to be delivered of coal-black children! The middle class might be wary, but nobles led the way, and where the highborn led commoners soon followed. Both beverages were consumed from quite small cups. Coffee cups had handles, but tea was often taken from handleless teabowls copied after the Oriental model.

Porcelain services for these drinks consisted of a teapot and/or coffeepot, a sugar bowl, a slop or waste basin and cups and saucers. Some had a tea jar (caddy) and milk jug; some, porcelain spoons. Trays were added later. Services called *cabarets* were used for serving one (*cabaret solitaire*) or two (*cabaret tête-à-tête*).

In addition to figures and tablewares, the collector of Meissen can choose among a whole range of small, highly decorative objects which in the eighteenth century, before the word came largely to mean children's playthings, were called toys: needle cases, toothpick cases, cane handles (some with compartments for snuff), scent bottles, ink bottles, sandboxes, hand bells, pipe bowls and pipe stoppers. Small pieces of jewelry, earrings for example, were made of porcelain, too.

Small boxes have a special place in the history of Meissen manufacturing, as they do in the history of all eighteenth-century European porcelain factories. They include patch boxes, for the patches that both sexes wore on their faces, jewel boxes, scent and pomade boxes and, above all, snuffboxes. Brühl, like many of his contemporaries, was a great lover of snuffboxes (he owned about seven hundred), and during his administration Meissen turned them out by the thousands.

All these objects, large or small, for use or display, were decorated with painting as high in quality as the modeling. The variety of decorative subjects is dizzying: some authorities claim there are literally no two pieces of Meissen painted alike.

The earliest decoration, in 1715–19, during the Böttger period, was straightforward copying of Ming and Ch'ing vase painting and the Kakiemon style of Japan. Plenty of examples for copying were at hand in Augustus the Strong's Oriental collection. European artisans did not of course understand what they were, to the best of their ability, copying. Many of the flowers shown on Chinese porcelain, for instance, were unknown in Europe, but the copying was so extraordinarily good that Meissen wares have been taken for Chinese. Straight duplication of Chinese motifs continued, but most soon became chinoiserie.

15.
Chinoiserie depictions of the imagined life in China (a mandarin strolling, followed by his umbrella of state; a Chinese child playing a cup-and-ball game) decorate Meissen jugs with pewter mounts. The painting is in the style of Johann Gregor Herold. German, about 1732–35. Height, with cover, of each: 19.6 cm. (7¾ in.). Mark: crossed swords in underglaze blue. Cooper-Hewitt Museum, gift of R. Thornton Wilson

Chinoiserie can be described as the Europeans' naive idea of what China ought to be. Europeans had almost no precise information about the Celestial Empire at the time, and what little they had they tended to romanticize, preferring to picture China as a land under benign rulership where life was simple, chaste and playful. Of course China, land of flood, famine and barbarian invasions, never resembled that picture, but Europeans portrayed it this way for years even after China was penetrated and became fairly well known to the West. Traces of chinoiserie are easy to find in decoration today: blue (or red) willowware is still on dinner tables all over the world. In chinoiserie decoration, Chinese-like figures are shown in countless situations and occupations in landscapes never seen in this or any other world (plate 15). Thousands, perhaps millions, of pieces of chinoiserie porcelain were painted at Meissen and other European factories in the eighteenth century, especially in the first half (see plate 30).

A specialty of Meissen painting was the "harbor scene" depicted on innumerable pieces around the middle of the eighteenth century (colorplate 1). These scenes show wharfs with merchandise heaped up along them and many little figures, vaguely Chinese or equally vaguely Turkish, busy with commerce among the bales. European quays were also depicted; then the pictures are known as Dutch harbor scenes. While much harbor-scene painting is fanciful, there are also many landscapes and townscapes that are quite authentic, derived mainly from topographical engravings of the time.

Many decorators of Meissen porcelain are known by name since, although rare, a number of signed pieces do exist. Johann Georg Heintze was one of the best-known harbor-scene painters. He was another of Meissen's rambunctious workmen. In 1748 he was put in prison for absenting himself without leave. Other famous and collected painters include the cousins Christian Friedrich Herold and Johann Gregor Herold (or Höroldt), both of whom excelled at chinoiserie harbor scenes. The latter became *Obermaler* (head painter) of the Meissen factory and in 1731 manager of all the factory's workers. His is one of the important names in the history of porcelain. Among other contributions, he greatly expanded the Meissen palette so that it included red, purple, turquoise and green. Blue came later, but was never used to any extent at Meissen because of its tendency to flake. During the eighteenth century the idea of *Fondporzellan*, pieces painted with an overall background color (the ground) with white spaces reserved (the reserves) for decoration, entered Meissen decoration (see colorplate 1). The technique has been used at many other factories since. The Meissen grounds include, among other colors, yellow, purple, red and brown, so collectors classify a piece as a "yellow ground teapot," for example. There was also striking decoration in monochrome black (*Schwarzlot*).

16.
A plate from the Meissen *Schwanenge-schirr* (Swan service), designed to serve at least one hundred diners. German, about 1737–41. Diameter: 37.3 cm. (14¾ in.). Mark: crossed swords in underglaze blue. Cooper-Hewitt Museum, purchased in memory of Commander Henry H. Gorringe

As already noted, Meissen floral painting at first was copied from imported wares and depicted *indianische Blumen* (Oriental flowers), many of which never grew in Europe. Later, more natural flowers, called *deutsche Blumen* (German flowers), were painted. Butterflies and other insects were frequently scattered over the pieces, sometimes at random but often deliberately to hide flaws in the glaze. Pastoral painting, in which typically a swain attempts to encircle the tiny waist of a shepherdess with his arms while a sheep looks on unconcernedly, was popular after about 1735–40.

The finest decoration was created for the great table services made at Meissen from the 1730s. They took their names from the subjects of decoration. Augustus the Strong had the Yellow Lion and Red Dragon services, both decorated in the Kakiemon style, and the Butterfly service, in chinoiserie, in the 1730s. Kändler and his assistant Eberlein created the celebrated Swan service for Brühl in 1737–41. This service was decorated with swans, gods and goddesses, shells, animals, water birds and flowers. All were modeled in white relief, to which were added floral painting and the Brühl coat of arms (plate 16).

Such services were enormous: the Swan service had more than

two thousand pieces. Various parts of this and other services have been dispersed through looting, theft and sale, so it is not unusual for individual pieces to come on the art market today.

By no means all the decoration on Meissen was done in the factory. Some undecorated porcelain found its way to other cities for painting (see plate 10). Much white ware was taken home by employees and painted there. Decorators who worked on their own account, at home or in studios, are referred to as *Hausmaler*. The names of many are known from their signatures on pieces, and today their work commands respect and high prices.

Meissen porcelain has been marked many ways in its long history. Pseudo-Chinese marks were used in the early days. About 1723–24 the initials *KPM* (Königliche Porzellanmanufaktur) and variants were painted on many pieces. In 1724 the celebrated crossed swords were introduced, the most famous mark in porcelain history and perhaps the most forged. The mark has varied considerably, and there have been numerous additions, some of them of obscure meaning. Pieces marked *AR* (Augustus Rex, for Augustus the Strong or his son Augustus III) were intended for royal use or as royal gifts and were naturally of the highest quality. Forgers have reproduced this mark.

By the mid-eighteenth century the great days of Meissen had passed. The factory never really recovered from the depredations of Frederick the Great of Prussia, who occupied Dresden in 1756 at the start of the Seven Years' War. The kilns were destroyed during the bombardment of the city, and most of the workmen (578 at the time) hastily decamped. Frederick, who wanted to revive the factory, leased it to a businessman to whom he gave substantial orders. The businessman rebuilt the kilns and hired new workers as well as rehiring some of the former employees. For several years Frederick was Meissen's most important customer. By the time the Prussian occupation ended and peace was made, the factory had regained its feet, but its spirit and the quality of its porcelain were never quite the same.

Starting in the late seventeenth century, European collectors began to display their Oriental porcelain in specially decorated rooms. It was customary to crowd the mantelpieces, shelves and niches in the walls with as many examples as possible, and the decoration of the entire room was often of chinoiserie design. Porcelain Room, Charlottenburg Palace, Berlin, 1703 (engraving)

5 Rococo Porcelain: Northern Europe

Meissen was the ancestor of many porcelain factories. Böttger's formula was called the "mystery" or, more frequently, the "arcanum" of hard-paste porcelain. A man who knew the process was an "arcanist." Closely guarded, the secret nevertheless slipped out, as workmen left surreptitiously for other cities where they either opened porcelain factories themselves or sold the arcanum at high prices to entrepreneurs.

The arcanum is said to have been divided among three people at Meissen, including Böttger, so that no one could bolt with the complete formula and make his own porcelain. There must have been a slipup, however, since Samuel Stölzel, who deserted in 1719, apparently had the secret complete and helped father the Vienna factory. He later returned to Meissen, bringing with him Johann Gregor Herold.

The Meissen factory was not the home of a happy band of master craftsmen working together to produce this beautiful new ware. Far from it. The factory was constantly beset with what today would be called "personality problems." Böttger was on such bad terms with so many of the workers that from the beginning the factory functioned with difficulty. Kirchner and Kändler could not get along, and Kirchner had to leave. Kändler and Herold hated each other and quarreled incessantly. When employees left the Meissen factory their departure was generally caused by dissension.

So the porcelain arcanum was transmitted in many ways, nearly all on the shady side of the law. The history of the spread of porcelain throughout central Europe in the eighteenth century is full of dramatic episodes in which defectors from Meissen were bribed, browbeaten or even kidnapped to obtain the secret. Rulers in central Europe were mad to have their own porcelain factories: they were an important embellishment, almost a necessity, of the princely state.

Colorplate 7.
Among Franz Anton Bustelli's Italian Comedy figures for the Nymphenburg factory none better typifies his style than Colombina (Columbine), one of the heroines. German, eighteenth century. Height: 22 cm. (8⅝ in.). Mark: shield on side of base, impressed and outlined in gold. Metropolitan Museum of Art, gift of R. Thornton Wilson, 1950, in memory of Florence Ellsworth Wilson

17

18

19

Because of the constant suborning of staff and the flitting of arcanists, painters and workmen from one factory to another, the same names recur in the history of eighteenth-century porcelain. A prominent example is Josef Jakob Ringler, who learned the secret of porcelain making while an apprentice at the Vienna factory. He wandered to Höchst in 1750, Strasbourg in 1751, Nymphenburg in 1753 and so on until 1759, when he became director of Ludwigsburg, a position that apparently suited him since he stayed there for forty years.

In the German-speaking world many porcelain factories were founded during the eighteenth century. Some were of short duration and their few products of interest only to highly specialized collectors. Those considered the most important are as follows:

VIENNA (1719–1864). Vienna, the second true-porcelain factory to be established in Europe, was founded by Claudius Innocentius Du Paquier with the assistance of Samuel Stölzel, who, as mentioned, had defected from Meissen. Du Paquier kept going with great financial difficulty until his factory was taken over by the Austrian state in 1744. The products of the Vienna factory are identified by the period of their production: Du Paquier 1719–44; First State 1744–84; Sorgenthal (after Konrad von Sorgenthal, the director) 1784–1805; Third State 1805–64. The rather scarce products of the Du Paquier period are the Vienna porcelains most sought by collectors (plates 17 and 18).

Despite its Meissen ancestry, Vienna's style is quite distinctive, and the decoration in particular owes less than might be thought to the mother factory. In its early days the decoration was elaborate and baroque in manner. A great deal of *Schwarzlot* painting with gilding, often chinoiserie, was used (plate 18). Formal abstract ornamentation is characteristic. Much of the decoration was done outside the factory by *Hausmaler*. Most collectors think that the best figures (crinoline, Italian Comedy, Callot, etc.) are those from the First State period.

Du Paquier porcelain is not marked. The Vienna shield mark began to be used in 1744 and with considerable variation was on the wares until the factory closed.

FÜRSTENBERG (1747 to the present). Established in Brunswick, the factory had a lot of trouble getting started. Although its patent goes back to 1747, it was not until after 1770, when it came under court direction, that its finest wares began to be produced. Very good Italian Comedy figures were made at Fürstenberg as well as the traditional series: Four Elements, Five Senses, Four Continents (plate 19), Greek Gods, Craftsmen and so forth. Decoration tended to be taken from books of engravings. Pictures on porcelain plaques with mythological or pastoral subjects were a Fürstenberg specialty. The mark was and remains a cursive *F*.

HÖCHST (1750–98). Located near Mainz in the Rhineland, the factory was established when Ringler brought the porcelain secret from Vienna. The body of Höchst porcelain is milky white. The figures are light and rococo, the subjects often Italian Comedy and peasant groups. The colors of the figures are delicate, the flesh having a distinctive pinkish tone (plate 20). Later designs were sentimental, inspired by the philosophy of Jean-Jacques Rousseau, especially in the small figures of children. There is a lot of chinoiserie in Höchst decoration (plate 21). A distinctive color is purple used with gold borders (plate 22).

For its mark Höchst often used a six-spoke wheel in red or another colored enamel. After Höchst closed, the molds were sold to other factories, and copies of the Höchst wares were made at various places in Germany during the nineteenth century.

NYMPHENBURG (1753 to the present). Not until after the arrival of the ubiquitous Ringler was porcelain made successfully at Nymphenburg, a suburb of Munich. Nymphenburg often is considered second only to Meissen in importance among German factories, and there

17.
Vienna mug with characteristic frieze of symmetrical arabesques and scene of woman and child playing musical instruments. Austrian, about 1730. Height: 8.2 cm. (3¼ in.). Unmarked. Cooper-Hewitt Museum, purchased in memory of Miss Eleanor Garnier Hewitt

18.
Vienna cup and saucer painted in *Schwarzlot* by Jacobus Helchis, one of the most noted practitioners of this form of decoration, and signed. Austrian, about 1730. Height of cup: 7 cm. (2¾ in.). Diameter of saucer: 14.5 cm. (5¾ in.). Unmarked; on bottom of saucer: signature *JH*. Cooper-Hewitt Museum, gift of R. Thornton Wilson

19.
Asia (right) and Africa from a Fürstenberg Four Continents set. German, late eighteenth century. Height: 16 cm. (6¼ in.). Mark: *F* in blue underglaze. Cooper-Hewitt Museum, gift of the Trustees of the Estate of James Hazen Hyde

20

21

20.
Höchst is noted for its many figures depicting a wide range of occupations and amusements. Woman in hunting dress holding a gun (missing). German, about 1755. Height: 15.3 cm. (6 in.). Unmarked. Smithsonian Institution, National Museum of History and Technology, gift of Mr. and Mrs. Edward M. Pflueger

21.
The Höchst figures include many in the chinoiserie style. Candleholder with seated Chinese figure. German, about 1755–60. Height: 19.1 cm. (7½ in.). Mark: wheel in red. Smithsonian Institution, National Museum of History and Technology, gift of Mr. and Mrs. Edward M. Pflueger

are collectors who prefer its work, especially its figures. The body of Nymphenburg porcelain, fine-grained and with very few flaws, has always been widely admired (plate 23).

The factory is invariably associated with the work of Franz Anton Bustelli, who as a modeler is ranked in a class with Kändler. A Swiss, Bustelli worked at the Nymphenburg factory from 1754 to 1763, the year of his death. He modeled the Four Seasons, Tradesmen and many other subjects, but he is perhaps most famous for his series of sixteen figures of the Italian Comedy, the renowned commedia dell'arte of Italy (colorplate 7). Traveling troupes of players, thought to be Italian in origin, were a familiar sight in seventeenth- and eighteenth-century Europe, and their performances enjoyed an amazing and persistent popularity. The players' wit, much of it improvised, was earthy, to say the least, and often obscene. They were given to grand, theatrical gestures, amply reflected in Bustelli's figures. Arlecchino (Harlequin), Pulcinella (still familiar today as Punch in Punch and Judy shows), Colombina (Columbine) and Pantalone (Pantaloon) were among the characters of the commedia dell'arte known to everyone. Kändler did dozens of Italian Comedy figures at Meissen, and other factories followed suit (see plates 33 and 60). Bustelli's remarkable figures in this series are today considered among the highest achievements of porcelain art. They were reproduced in the late nineteenth century and again in this century; the originals are much sought after and sell for very high prices.

In addition to his masterwork figures, Bustelli, like other great modelers of the time, made many toys, the small decorative objects so characteristic of the eighteenth century. There is no indication that

22.
Höchst teapot painted in purple with allegorical scenes of Africa and America after Jacopo Amiconi in polychrome and gilt. German, about 1765. Height: 9.8 cm. (3⅞ in.). Mark: *IM* impressed underglaze, crowned. Cooper-Hewitt Museum, gift of the Trustees of the Estate of James Hazen Hyde

22

23.
Nymphenburg teapot and cover with scene of Mercury appearing to a woman. German, about 1760. Height: 11.7 cm. (4⅝ in.). Marks: shield, impressed, and number *111* in circle. Cooper-Hewitt Museum, purchased in memory of the Misses Hewitt

23

24

25

24.
Fanciful figures with cherubs and various gentle birds and animals were popular at many factories in the second half of the eighteenth century. Among Frankenthal's large figural production are such examples as this seminude woman with two doves and a cherub. German, about 1760. Height: 24.2 cm. (9½ in.). Marks: lion in underglaze blue and incised initials *PH*, for Paul Hannong, director of the Frankenthal factory at the time. Smithsonian Institution, National Museum of History and Technology

he or other modelers considered such items frivolous or beneath their talents, and they lavished all their skills on them.

The Nymphenburg mark was a shield in the eighteenth century, to which a crown was added in the nineteenth century. A few of Bustelli's works are marked *FB* or merely *B*.

FRANKENTHAL (1755–1800). Established in 1755, the factory at Frankenthal, a town near Mannheim, was purchased in 1762 by the local prince, the Elector Palatine, Carl Theodor. A great range of items was made at Frankenthal, including charming *cabarets* with richly painted diamond- or lozenge-shaped trays, clock cases, mirror frames and chessmen. The painting—chinoiserie, classical subjects, hunting scenes—was on a high level.

Of the greatest interest to collectors are the more than eight hundred different figures known to have been modeled at Frankenthal (plate 24). The usual series of subjects prevailed, plus music parties, toilet scenes showing court ladies at their dressing tables and ballet dancers. After the factory closed in 1800, the molds went to various other factories, especially Nymphenburg, where the figures were reproduced.

Frankenthal porcelain was marked with the lion or shield of the arms of the Palatinate. From 1762 to 1793 the usual mark was the crowned monogram of the Elector Carl Theodor. All these marks were painted on the porcelain in underglaze blue.

LUDWIGSBURG (1758–1824). Ringler, as noted above, was director of this factory from 1759 to 1799. It was organized and closely supervised by the local prince, Carl Eugen, Duke of Württemberg, who like so many of his fellow rulers was porcelain mad. His descendants kept the factory going until 1824, but its great days were the 1760s and 1770s. Among its popular figures were young couples in costume (plate 25) and ballet dancers; the factory also produced folk types and Italian Comedy figures, many of which have been copied and reproduced.

Until about 1793 the Ludwigsburg mark was interlaced C's, for the duke's initial, sometimes with a crown. After 1793 a stag's horn from the arms of Württemberg was used.

BERLIN (1761 to the present). This factory is closely associated with Frederick the Great. A financier named Johann Ernst Gotzkowsky purchased the arcanum in 1761 and made porcelain until 1763, when Frederick bought him out. The king, always a lover of fine china, had previously backed Wilhelm Kasper Wegely in making porcelain from 1752 to 1757 but had been dissatisfied with the results. He took a deep personal interest in his new porcelain factory, and a number of Meissen workmen were brought to Berlin at his orders.

25.
Ludwigsburg's many notable figures include pairs of men and women, often in rustic costume (as the woman is here). The man is masked, showing the two are probably dressed for a masquerade. German, about 1760. Height of woman: 13.2 cm. (5¼ in.); of man: 13.3 cm. (5¼ in.). Marks: woman marked with double C (for Duke Carl Eugen) and crown in blue; man with double C only. Both with incised initials and numerals (probably indicating models) as well. Cooper-Hewitt Museum, bequest of Mrs. Richard Irvin

26.
Berlin platter simply painted with floral sprays, a specialty of the factory. German, about 1770. Length: 36.8 cm. (14½ in.). Mark: scepter in underglaze blue. Smithsonian Institution, National Museum of History and Technology, Dr. Hans Syz Collection

26

Never one for half measures, Frederick passed stringent laws against the importation of porcelain so that his Prussian subjects would be obliged to get their china from his factory.

The Berlin porcelain body is a cold white, the decoration for the most part is in strong-colored enamels. Fine flower painting is characteristic (plate 26), and, as might be expected from a Prussian establishment, so are military and battle scenes, some surprisingly realistic (colorplate 8). The brothers Friedrich Elias Meyer and Wilhelm Christian Meyer were noted figure modelers in this factory.

Frederick commissioned large services from the factory as gifts to fellow princes. During one of their infrequent truces he gave Empress Catherine the Great of Russia a dessert service, curiously enough decorated with battle scenes, together with a table decoration of no fewer than forty figures, all made at his own factory and modeled by the Meyer brothers, representing the glorification of Catherine by the people of Russia.

The Berlin mark from 1763 was a scepter; the initials *KPM* (Königliche Porzellanmanufaktur) were added in the nineteenth century. Under the name Staatliche Porzellanmanufaktur, the Berlin factory is still in existence and still owned by the German state.

FULDA (1764–90) was well known for the quality of its figures (see frontispiece). The factory was established in Fulda by the bishop of the small German city and always had ecclesiastical backing. Those auspices show in the Fulda mark, which until about 1780 carried a cross. Then two *F*'s, sometimes crowned, were used.

Although these are the major factories, northern Europe boasted a few other important factories, outside Germany and Austria, whose wares are collected. They are described below.

ST. PETERSBURG (IMPERIAL FACTORY) (1744–1917). This factory's initial results were hardly promising: the first arcanist is said to have spent four years making just six imperfect cups. Catherine the Great became closely involved with the factory from 1762 onward, and her imperial patronage brought success. Most of the wares were basically French in style although many were painted with Russian views. Russian figures were also made. Enormous services for royalty were the bedrock of the enterprise. Although the factory's mark changed many times during the factory's history, the initial of each successive ruler, beginning with Catherine the Great, was usually present. The St. Petersburg porcelain (plate 27) is rare in the West.

Another Russian factory, the GARDNER, was founded near Moscow in 1766 by an English family, the Gardners, who controlled it until 1891. It produced fine services in the eighteenth century, but its best pieces are from the nineteenth. The initial *G* or the name *Gardner* in Latin or Cyrillic letters were frequent marks.

Colorplate 8.
Berlin coffee service showing coffeepot, milk jug, sugar bowl, cups and saucers decorated in relief and with overglaze polychrome battle scenes. German, after 1763. Height of coffeepot: 21.4 cm. (8⅜ in.). Height of milk jug: 14 cm. (5½ in.). Mark: scepter in underglaze blue on all pieces. Cooper-Hewitt Museum, bequest of Georgiana L. McClellan

27

28

27.
Russian porcelains were always noted for painting in vivid colors. From the Imperial Factory at St. Petersburg, this is one of a pair of vases with flame finials that can be reversed to form candleholders. Russian, about 1760. Height with candleholder: 19.7 cm. (7¾ in.). Mark: circled dot impressed underglaze. Metropolitan Museum of Art, gift of R. Thornton Wilson, 1954, in memory of Florence Ellsworth Wilson

Z

Russian porcelains—and there were other factories besides the St. Petersburg and the Gardner—are brilliantly decorated and, although owing much to Europe, have a distinctly Russian character.

ZURICH (1763–91). The first porcelain made at Zurich was soft-paste, but kaolin was brought to the factory from outside Switzerland in 1765, and in the next decade the factory produced some extraordinarily fine hard-paste, mainly table services, candlesticks, snuffboxes and perfume bottles, and a number of lovely rustic figures, which are collected today (plate 28). Since there were no princes in Switzerland, Zurich had the unusual distinction on the Continent of being run by a private business combine from beginning to end. The mark was a Z in blue.

COPENHAGEN (about 1772 to the present). Queen Juliana Maria of Denmark inspired this important factory, whose range of products encompassed nearly all those mentioned at the other factories, vases included (plate 29), plus toilet sets, mirror frames, brush backs, buttons and plaques. The word "Royal" was added to its name in 1779.

After Meissen's Swan service, probably the most famous eighteenth-century porcelain service is Royal Copenhagen's Flora Danica, which is decorated, with matchless scientific accuracy and beauty, with the native plants of Denmark. Originally intended as a gift from the Danish royal family to Catherine the Great, it was unfinished at the time of her death. A German-born artist named Johann Christoph Bayer did nearly all the painting—and ruined his eyesight doing so. Work began on the service in about 1789–90, and when it stopped in 1802 the service was still incomplete even though 1602 pieces had been painted. Unlike many other great porcelain services, the Flora Danica has never been broken up and remains in the possession of the Danish crown. A very few pieces have been given to museums, and some examples are being reproduced at present.

The factory's original mark of three wavy lines in blue (representing the three principal Danish waterways) has been retained to this day, with a crown and other variations added through the years.

28.
Boy Playing the Flute, one of the simple figures of great charm that were a specialty of the Zurich factory. Swiss, about 1770. Height: 13.4 cm. (5¼ in.). Unmarked. Smithsonian Institution, National Museum of History and Technology, Dr. Hans Syz Collection

29.
Pair of covered vases from the Copenhagen factory. Danish, about 1772. Height of each: 36.8 cm. (14½ in.). Mark: wavy mark in underglaze blue. Smithsonian Institution, National Museum of History and Technology, gift of Harris Masterson

29

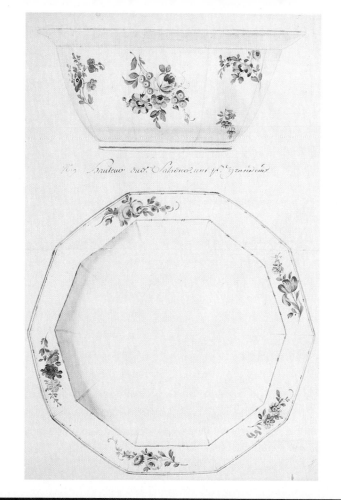

Hauteur dud. Salière, au ½ de grandeur

6 Rococo Porcelain: Italy, Spain and France

The lamentable failure of the sixteenth-century Medici porcelain offered little encouragement to later Italian potters. More than a century and a half passed before the success of Meissen and Vienna tempted Italians to try again to make porcelain. Happily, the results this time were more than satisfactory.

Hard-paste porcelain was made very briefly at Venice between 1720 and 1730, when the Vezzi family employed a workman from Meissen, Christoph Konrad Hunger (who also worked at Vienna, Copenhagen and St. Petersburg), to teach them the porcelain secret. The VEZZI factory was actually the third in Europe, after Meissen and Vienna, to make true porcelain. Kaolin was brought from Aue in Germany. The best of Vezzi can be compared to the earlier products of Meissen and Vienna, although the quality was uneven and the color of the paste uncertain. Vezzi was painted in polychrome or monochrome with chinoiseries (plate 30) and heraldic designs and marked *Venezia* or *Ven.ª* Vezzi, which is rare, has been widely forged.

Another Venetian factory, COZZI (plates 31 and 32), had an extensive production between 1764 and 1812. Geminiano Cozzi's license from the city specifically permitted him to manufacture "porcelain in the Japanese style," showing that porcelain continued to be associated in the European mind with the Orient after half a century of European manufacture. Cozzi was soft-paste, decorated sometimes in the European manner, sometimes in the Far Eastern, and marked with an anchor in red. Not rare like Vezzi, Cozzi has a strong following of collectors.

DOCCIA, Florence's famous manufactory, has made porcelain since 1737 (plate 34). The factory was founded by the Marchese Carlo Ginori, and the Ginori family is still associated with it. The early paste, actually a kind of hybrid hard-paste, was soft and grayish with elaborate decoration and heavy relief. Tablewares, centerpieces

Venezia.

Colorplates 9 and 10.
Very few examples are known of the original drawings for eighteenth-century porcelain design. Those from the French porcelain factory at Sèvres are especially rare, and it is therefore notable that the Cooper-Hewitt Museum has in its possession the pencil and watercolor design for a Sèvres salad bowl as well as the porcelain bowl made from it. The painting on the porcelain is by Jacques Michaud, who was active as a Sèvres painter from 1757 to 1780. Drawing: 41.7 x 31 cm. (16⅜ x 12¼ in.). Height of salad bowl: 11.3 cm. (4⅜ in.). Marks: crossed L's with datemark K (for 1763) in underglaze blue. Cooper-Hewitt Museum, gift of Mrs. John Jay Ide, in memory of John Jay Ide

30

31

30.

The first Italian factory to make true porcelain was the Vezzi in Venice, which began operations early in the eighteenth century with decoration in the popular chinoiserie style. Vezzi vase with cover. Italian, about 1725–30. Height: 28.6 cm. (11¼ in.). Unmarked. Metropolitan Museum of Art, gift of R. Thornton Wilson, 1950, in memory of Florence Ellsworth Wilson

31.

The Cozzi factory in Venice frequently worked in the Meissen style, but in soft-paste. Tea service with painted views of Italian villas. The monogram *GA*, shown on the cup at left, is painted in floral wreaths and probably indicates the first owner. Italian, about 1765. Height of teapot: 11.5 cm. (4½ in.). Diameter of each saucer: 11.8 cm. (4⅝ in.). Mark: red anchor. Smithsonian Institution, National Museum of History and Technology, Dr. Hans Syz Collection

and miniature figures were among the products, the best dating from 1748 to 1791—the second of the several periods into which the wares are divided—when the factory was managed by Lorenzo Ginori and the original recipe was altered and greatly improved. Doccia marks are extremely complicated: a star with varying numbers of points was used in the eighteenth century, the Ginori name in many different forms in the nineteenth and twentieth.

The collecting of early Doccia ware has experienced a revival in recent years. Collectors do not always feel entirely comfortable with this early ware, however, because of the factory's long history of using discarded molds of many factories, often complete with the old marks. Doccia has also imitated Chinese and Japanese porcelain and made majolica (tin-glazed earthenware) and other kinds of pottery. The factory began making reproductions around 1820; some of these now have the discolorations and cracks of age, which makes them difficult to distinguish from the original pieces.

The porcelain made at CAPODIMONTE between 1743 and 1759 (plate 33) is today considered the finest Italian porcelain, representing a reversal of earlier taste. Only a generation ago few ceramic authorities thought much of Capodimonte. Writers dismissed the wares almost cavalierly, one scholar noting only that the figures of Capodimonte's most famous modeler, Giuseppe Gricci, had "heads too small for their bodies." Now Capodimonte—especially Gricci's rare figures—sells for exceedingly high prices, a prime example of the changing fashions in collecting.

32.
Figure of dwarf after the engravings of
Jacques Callot, from the Cozzi factory,
Venice. Italian, about 1770. Height: 8.3
cm. (3¾ in.). Unmarked. Metropolitan
Museum of Art, gift of R. Thornton Wil-
son, 1950, in memory of Florence Ells-
worth Wilson

33.
Capodimonte is particularly noted for
its rare, strongly modeled figures. Pantalone (Pantaloon), a character in the
Italian Comedy series. Italian, about 1750–
52. Height: 22 cm. (8⅝ in.). Unmarked.
Metropolitan Museum of Art, gift of
R. Thornton Wilson, 1950, in memory
of Florence Ellsworth Wilson

34.
Doccia coffeepot decorated with landscape medallions in red violet. Italian,
about 1780–1800. Height: 21.8 cm. (8½
in.). Mark: five-pointed star in red
violet. Cooper-Hewitt Museum, gift of
George B. and Georgiana L. McClellan

32

33

34

Capodimonte is a royal palace in Naples, and it was there that the factory was established in 1743 under the eyes of its founder, the Bourbon King Charles IV of Naples, and his queen, a granddaughter of Augustus the Strong who had brought quantities of Meissen porcelain in her dowry. The factory worked largely for the court. A soft-paste porcelain, Capodimonte is esteemed for its milky beauty—one writer has described it as "almost edible."

Gricci was the chief and best-known modeler. His specialties included such religious objects as madonnas, pietàs and holy water stoups and such toys as snuffboxes in the form of monkeys and mythological figures. Gricci was in charge when the factory created for the king an entire room (still displayed at the Museo di Capodimonte, Naples) covered with porcelain panels with high relief and exuberantly decorated in chinoiserie.

Capodimonte was rather indifferently marked but usually carried the armorial fleur-de-lis of the Bourbon family.

Charles IV, King of Naples, became Charles III, King of Spain, in 1759. He was so fond of his Capodimonte porcelain that he packed up the factory, workers and all, and took it with him to Madrid. The numbers and job classifications of the staff who emigrated afford a glimpse into the management of an eighteenth-century porcelain factory. Nineteen modelers, two throwers, one carver, ten kiln workers, four color grinders, one gold beater, fourteen painters and one mounter were on the staff. Giuseppe Gricci went along to become chief modeler, now signing his work José Gricci.

The new Spanish factory was also in the royal palace grounds and also took its name from the palace, in this case, BUEN RETIRO. The

35.
The tradition of figure making was brought along when the Capodimonte factory moved from Naples to Madrid and took the name Buen Retiro. Boy with bunches of purple grapes from Buen Retiro. Spanish, about 1765–70. Height: 21.6 cm. (8½ in.). Mark: *K* in brown overglaze. Smithsonian Institution, National Museum of History and Technology, Dr. Hans Syz Collection

earliest Buen Retiro porcelain, which was soft-paste, dates from about 1760. The factory made elaborate tablewares, centerpieces (fountains to flow with wine, among them) and flowers. Many fine figures, now rare, were made (plate 35). Like Capodimonte, Buen Retiro sometimes used the Bourbon fleur-de-lis as its mark. The factory began to make hard-paste in 1804, but shut its doors in 1808.

A dozen years after the Capodimonte factory departed for Spain, another porcelain establishment opened in Naples, under the patronage of Charles's son Ferdinand IV. Referred to as NAPLES, it produced soft-paste porcelain of no particular distinction. The colorful painted decoration included views of the city, Vesuvius (erupting), Neapolitan peasants (plate 36) and the inevitable birds, fish and flowers. Figures were in local costumes. Large table services showed the ruins of the recently rediscovered Roman cities of Herculaneum and Pompeii. The Naples factory went into decline in the late 1700s, but was not finally defunct until 1834. The mark was a crowned N, and occasionally RF, for Rex Ferdinandus. Today, porcelain made by the Naples factory and its later imitators is frequently and erroneously called Capodimonte.

Soft-paste porcelains are among the most important manifestations of French eighteenth-century taste. At ST. CLOUD, outside Paris, soft-paste manufacturing by the Chicanneau and Trou families had begun perhaps as early as 1677, a generation before Böttger managed to make true porcelain at Meissen. St. Cloud is highly translucent, with an ivory color, and the surface of the glaze is noticeably pitted.

36.
Two plates from the Naples factory, showing costumes of the kingdom. The figures on the left wear the dress of the Massagrognia region; those on the right, the Triventi. Italian, about 1820. Diameter of each plate: 23.2 cm. (9⅛ in.). Unmarked. Smithsonian Institution, National Museum of History and Technology, Dr. Hans Syz Collection

The good proportions of St. Cloud forms are much admired. Many small objects were made for domestic use: dressing-table necessities such as pomade pots; spice boxes with three compartments for various spices; potpourri vases, which were pierced vessels for holding fragrant leaves and herbs; and pastille burners. (A pastille was an aromatic substance burned like incense.) Sanitation being what it was, there was ample use for potpourris and pastille burners in the eighteenth century. The forms were often unexpected—a pastille burner in the shape of a cat, for example. The tablewares, on the other hand, were in simple, practical forms (plate 37).

St. Cloud's decoration included chinoiserie; the factory's "Chinamen" (generally plump, laughing figures remotely derived from Chinese mythology) were especially saucy and engaging. When glazed but undecorated, they closely—and intentionally—resembled the imported *blanc de chine* figures which were especially popular in France.

From about 1695 to 1722 the St. Cloud mark was a sunburst. The initials *St. C.*, occasionally with a *T* for the Trou family, succeeded this and were used until the factory closed in 1766. The decline in its business after midcentury was due to competition from the thriving Sèvres factory, which enjoyed royal patronage and direct subsidy.

37

38

39

37.
The soft-paste porcelain of the St. Cloud factory lent itself beautifully to relief decoration, as in this covered custard cup. French, second quarter of the eighteenth century. Height: 7.5 cm. (2⅞ in.). Mark: *St. C.* impressed. Cooper-Hewitt Museum, gift of Catherine Oglesby

38.
The Kakiemon style was often used at the Chantilly factory, and its products in this style have seldom been surpassed by any other European porcelain factory. The cup and saucer each have a bird of paradise in overglaze iron red, light green and blue enamels. French, about 1740. Height of cup: 6.8 cm. (2⅝ in.). Diameter of saucer: 12.8 cm. (5 in.). Mark: hunting horn in red. Cooper-Hewitt Museum, gift of Mrs. Morris Hawkes

39.
The *écuelle* (covered bowl) with stand is a highly characteristic form of French eighteenth-century porcelain. Chantilly *écuelle* and stand decorated in the Kakiemon style. French, eighteenth century. Height of bowl with cover: 10 cm. (3⅞ in.). Length of stand: 24 cm. (9½ in.). Mark: hunting horn in red. Cooper-Hewitt Museum

(See below for an extended discussion of the famous factory at Sèvres.)

Louis-Henri de Bourbon, Prince de Condé, a devotee of Japanese porcelain, established a soft-paste porcelain factory in his palace at CHANTILLY, near Paris, in 1725. Chantilly ware, which somewhat resembles St. Cloud, is markedly translucent. The decoration, at first copied directly from the prince's collection of Far Eastern porcelain, gradually became more naturalistic and European. But Chantilly's

40

42

41

.D.V.

40.
Floral decoration in relief was used frequently at the Mennecy factory. Covered jar in acorn shape, with floral festoons in relief on shoulders and flowers in relief on cover, which has a silver rim. French, about 1740–50. Height: 12.1 cm. (4¾ in.). Mark: *DV*, for the Duc de Villeroy, patron of the factory, incised underglaze. Cooper-Hewitt Museum, gift of Mrs. Edward Luckemeyer

41.
Étuis, small cases for holding sewing necessities like needles and scissors, were often made in porcelain in fruit or vegetable forms. Mennecy *étui* in asparagus form; the metal cover contains a cameo seal. French, eighteenth century. Length: 11.2 cm. (4⅜ in.). Unmarked. Cooper-Hewitt Museum, gift of Norvin Hewitt Green

42.
The French mounted both imported Chinese porcelain and their own soft-paste products in ormolu. In many cases, as here, the porcelain was a French imitation of *blanc de chine*. Pair of Mennecy Chinese figures transformed into candelabra. French, about 1750. Overall height of each figure, including ormolu: 31 cm. (12¼ in.). Unmarked. Cooper-Hewitt Museum

most characteristic decoration remained Kakiemon designs: Japanese flowers; a squirrel eating a nut; a stork, a partridge or a bird of paradise (plate 38); a butterfly or a beetle (plate 39). The style is extremely restrained, with simple reds, blues, greens and yellows predominating. Strong colors were seldom used. The factory also specialized in little painted bouquets of flowers called Chantilly sprigs, which were later copied at the English factories of Caughley, Derby and Worcester. Very few figures were made at Chantilly. The factory, after surviving competition from Sèvres for three-quarters of a century, finally closed in 1800.

The Chantilly mark is particularly charming, a hunting horn in red or blue. Occasionally a piece has an artist's mark. Chantilly porcelain, especially that of the early period painted in the Kakiemon style, is extremely popular with collectors in Europe.

From 1734 to about 1785 soft-paste porcelain was also made at MENNECY, on the outskirts of Paris. The factory moved several times but remained in the Paris vicinity. The wares are the same general type as St. Cloud and Chantilly. The forms are simple and often decorated with flowers in relief (plate 40). Mennecy made a wide variety of articles, including tablewares, vases, small receptacles (plate 41) and figures. The light and refined figures were Orientals (plate 42 —the ormolu on the pieces shown in the plate was added later), children playing instruments, Italian Comedy characters and Callot dwarfs. Meissen obviously inspired many of these subjects. Like that of other French soft-paste porcelain, much of Mennecy's charm lies in the restraint of its decoration: a delicate palette, with pink and blue prominent, was employed. A few portrait busts were made in white porcelain. Mennecy was marked *DV*, for the Duc de Villeroy, patron of the factory.

Technically, the porcelain made at TOURNAI from 1751 can be considered French soft-paste even though the city belonged to the Austrian crown when maufacture began and is now part of Belgium. A number of the first workers came from Chantilly and Vincennes (see below), and the wares are related to the products of these establishments. The factory was successful and production large.

Collectors think the Tournai porcelain of the period 1762–81, when it had a warm tone similar to that of Sèvres, is the best. The decoration included birds and landscapes, grisaille (monochrome gray) painting in medallions, and blue-and-white (a late appearance of this Chinese combination on the European scene). Some white china was sent to The Hague to be decorated.

Tournai was one of the few major European porcelain manufactories of the eighteenth century to supply utilitarian wares destined for use in middle-class households (plate 43).

Between 1751 and 1756 Tournai's mark was a tower, a play on

43.
The simple but elegantly made Tournai blue-and-white was eminently suitable for use on the tables of the non-princely. Soup plate. Belgian, about 1760. Diameter: 22.9 cm. (9 in.). Marks: crossed daggers with crosses in underglaze blue and incised *M*. Smithsonian Institution, National Museum of History and Technology, Alfred Duane Pell Collection

44.
Three examples of the celebrated porcelain flowers made at the Vincennes factory. French, about 1748. Diameter of each flower: 5.1 cm. (2 in.). Unmarked. Smithsonian Institution, National Museum of History and Technology, Dr. Hans Syz Collection

43

44

45.
The Sèvres factory made many dinner, tea and coffee services despite the fact that the expensive soft-paste porcelain was subject to chipping and staining. Soup plate decorated with floral sprays and gilding. French, about 1770. Diameter: 22.5 cm. (8⅞ in.). Marks: crossed *L*'s in overglaze blue and initials of various workmen. Cooper-Hewitt Museum, bequest of Mrs. John Innes Kane

46.
Monteith used for rinsing and chilling wine glasses. One of a pair from Sèvres. French, about 1770. Overall length: 29.6 cm. (11⅝ in.). Marks: crossed *L*'s in overglaze blue with initials of workmen incised underglaze. Cooper-Hewitt Museum, bequest of Mrs. John Innes Kane

47.
Many small and elegant objects for the elaborate eighteenth-century dressing table were made at Sèvres. Pair of pomade jars. French, about 1756. Height of each: 6.7 cm. (2⅝ in.). Mark: decorator's mark of Charles Tandart the Younger. Metropolitan Museum of Art, gift of R. Thornton Wilson, 1950, in memory of Florence Ellsworth Wilson

the city's name. The best pieces are said to be marked in gold. From 1756 to 1781 the mark was two crossed daggers with crosses in the corners, and sometimes incised initials, probably of workmen. Many pieces of Tournai, however, were unmarked. The factory finally closed its doors in 1891.

Not a few connoisseurs believe that the queen of porcelain factories is SÈVRES. For more than two centuries its porcelain, especially the soft-paste, has been collected and studied, one of the few porcelains never to go out of fashion. Vincennes, a suburb of Paris, was the original home of the factory, which in 1756 moved to Sèvres, also a Paris suburb. The porcelain produced was the same at both locations, but it is customary to distinguish the wares as Vincennes (before 1756) and Sèvres (after).

When the production of soft-paste porcelain began at VIN-CENNES in 1738, the factory was ostensibly a private enterprise, but King Louis XV made a large contribution to its capital and permitted the founders to use the palace at Vincennes as their workshop.

The Vincennes specialty was porcelain flowers, which accounted for about eighty percent of the value of the factory's sales (plate 44). The flowers were true to nature in size and color. They were displayed in two ways: mounted on wire stems and shown as bouquets in vases (also made at the factory) or used in the decoration of other objects in the manner of Meissen flowers. The French royal family was indefatigable in promoting these very expensive items. The high point was an order filled in 1748–49 for the Dauphine of France for a bouquet of no fewer than 480 porcelain flowers in an ormolu vase to send to her father, the king of Saxony. This was not just a gesture of daughterly devotion; the Dauphine meant to advertise the Vincennes wares. Madame de Pompadour, Louis XV's mistress, adored flowers and was also an enthusiastic customer for the porcelain bouquets. On occasion she mixed these with real blooms and had them perfumed!

In 1753 Louis XV, with the encouragement of Madame de Pompadour, took more or less complete charge of Vincennes. The newly named Manufacture Royale de Porcelaine de France thereupon adopted as its official mark the intertwined, or crossed, L's of the king's monogram it was already using. The factory received a royal subsidy, and restrictions were placed on the production of porcelain at other French establishments. Not surprisingly, as has been noted, the other factories faded away. Every year after 1758 new china from Sèvres was exhibited in the palace of Versailles. Under the eyes of the king the courtiers had to look over the wares and purchase heavily. The king himself sometimes acted as head salesman. The courtiers bowed and bought, but, because of the inordinate expense, there was considerable grumbling out of earshot of the king and Madame de Pompadour.

Many table services, state and private, were made under Louis XV

48.
Sèvres condiment tray with two covered pots. French, about 1770. Length of tray: 25 cm. (9⅞ in.). Overall height of each pot: 8.5 cm. (3⅜ in.). Marks: overglaze obliterated, incised mark underglaze. Cooper-Hewitt Museum, bequest of Mrs. John Innes Kane

49.
Sèvres *écuelle* with stand used as a covered vegetable dish; handle of cover in the form of an olive branch. French, about 1770. Diameter of bowl: 13 cm. (5⅛ in.). Length of stand: 22.7 cm. (8⅞ in.). Mark: crossed L's in underglaze blue. Cooper-Hewitt Museum, gift of Mrs. John B. Trevor

(colorplates 9 and 10, plates 45 and 46). In addition, Sèvres made tea services (the earliest with bowl-shaped cups), pomade jars (plate 47), pastille burners, flowerpots, trays (plate 48), potpourri vases in the shape of ships called *vaisseaux à mât* (now extremely rare and expensive) and other forms. Bowls with covers and stands are highly characteristic (plate 49). Clock cases became staggeringly elaborate, their ormolu mounts hung with brilliants. Some forms, although magnificently crafted and colored, are rather trying to twentieth-century taste—for example, large vases with elephant heads at either side, the elephants' trunks serving as candleholders!

The glory of Sèvres is the color of its decoration, especially the famous ground colors—among them yellow, violet, deep green and light green. The technical direction at Vincennes and Sèvres from 1745 was under Jean Hellot of the French Academy of Sciences. He was a chemist and an expert on colors. *Bleu céleste* (turquoise) was introduced as a ground color by Hellot in 1752 at Vincennes. Perhaps the most famous color was *rose Pompadour*, an exquisite pink also invented by Hellot and used for about ten years beginning in 1757. For unfathomable reasons the English, confusing royal mistresses, call this color *rose du Barry*. A deep underglaze blue, introduced in 1759 and imitated at English factories, was called in England *mazarine blue*. *Bleu de roi*, a strong blue, came into use after midcentury (colorplate 11). These are only a few of Sèvres's remarkable group of colors; brown, purple and a gray-blue called *bleu turc* were also among the riches of the palette. Some of these were used *en camaïeu*, several shades of one color used on a single piece.

Scenes, birds and flowers were painted in the reserves of these splendid grounds. The chinoiseries, pastoral scenes and landscapes common to other European factories are found in these reserves, but more characteristic is flower painting, a specialty of Sèvres (plates 50 and 52). A great deal of gilding was applied, sometimes lightly, at other times heavily and burnished, giving an extraordinarily rich effect. In the 1780s, under Louis XVI, a type of Sèvres was made in which small drops of enamels were dotted over the gilding (or silvering) to achieve a "jeweled" look. Rare examples have bits of glass simulating jewels actually stuck onto the painting.

The Sèvres biscuit was itself so lovely that it was tempting to use it without decoration. After 1757 a whole series of biscuit figures by Étienne-Maurice Falconet, who worked at the factory, were made—children engaged in various activities (plate 51), dancers, mythological groups. Similar figures were also made in the manner of François Boucher. Many busts of famous people were executed in biscuit, including Jean-Jacques Rousseau and Voltaire. Very few Sèvres figures have any colored decoration.

The system of marks at Sèvres is unique. It was the first factory to adopt a mark that dated the piece. The Vincennes crossed *L*'s

Colorplate 11.
Sèvres vase, one of a pair, decorated in the famous *bleu de roi* ground with fine painted reserves of birds. Height: 19.2 cm. (7½ in.). Marks: crossed *L*'s with datemark *F* (for 1758) in underglaze blue. Metropolitan Museum of Art, gift of R. Thornton Wilson, 1954, in memory of Florence Ellsworth Wilson

50.
More painters at the Sèvres factory near Paris were employed to work on flowers than on any other subject. Plate with brilliant green *marli* (rim), with polychrome flowers in oval reserves, and, in the center, two birds in a grove. Diameter: 25.7 cm. (10⅛ in.). Marks: crossed L's with datemark *E* (for 1757) in overglaze blue. Cooper-Hewitt Museum, gift of Mr. and Mrs. Benjamin M. Reeves

continued to be used at Sèvres from 1756 to 1793, when the republic came into being, making a royal cipher no longer acceptable. In 1753 the factory began using letters of the alphabet to indicate the year in which the piece was made. The datemark for that year was *A*; for 1754, *B*; and so on. The first alphabet ran out in 1777, there being no *W* in French, and double letters were then employed: *AA* in 1778, *BB* in 1779, until 1793 (*PP*). From 1793 to 1800, *RF* (*République française*) was used, and from 1801 to 1817, a series of date signs, such as *oz* (*onze*, eleven) for 1811. The biscuit is not marked.

Still other marks are found on Sèvres porcelain. Artists who painted the wares signed their initials or drew a tiny sketch (an anchor, for example, was the sign of Charles Buteux *aîné*, figure painter), stars, crosses or whatever the artist fancied. Modelers and repairers also signed, usually with their initials. Collectors find the study of these marks as fascinating as that of the equally intricate marks on Chinese porcelain.

Charts explaining the Sèvres marks are given in many reference books. Collectors should be warned, however, that the marks have been reproduced in varying forms. Nor is there universal agreement as to which artist used which device as his signature. Because there has been extensive forging of Sèvres marks, attribution of a piece to the factory must rest on style and quality of form and decoration as well as the mark. Categories of forgeries include Sèvres marks that have been supplied on pieces made at another factory, nineteenth-century marks tampered with to make the piece appear to be eighteenth century and outright fakes produced fully marked. Examination under shortwave ultraviolet light will often disclose manipulation of the mark.

51.
Étienne-Maurice Falconet, noted for his full-size sculpture in marble, also modeled groups which were produced in Sèvres biscuit porcelain. *The Schoolmistress.* French, about 1762. Unmarked. Height: 21.2 cm. (8⅜ in.). Metropolitan Museum of Art, gift of R. Thornton Wilson, 1954, in memory of Florence Ellsworth Wilson

52.
Far more than any other eighteenth-century porcelain factory, the French factory of Sèvres produced porcelain that could be incorporated into pieces of furniture including desks, tables and secretaries. Serpentine sprays of flowers and foliage decorate a plaque meant for such a purpose. Length: 21.9 cm. (8⅝ in.). Marks: crossed *L*'s with datemark *N* (for 1766) in underglaze blue. Cooper-Hewitt Museum, bequest of Erskine Hewitt

7 Rococo Porcelain: England

The majority of Continental porcelain factories were inspired and sustained by the patronage of princes. The beginnings of porcelain in England were quite different. No princely sponsorship was bestowed on the English factories, except for a vague interest on the part of the royal Duke of Cumberland in the Chelsea factory. It was solely private enterprise, operated by middle-class entrepreneurs, that got the industry started.

The English were not exactly quick off the mark in beginning to manufacture porcelain. Not until the 1740s, when several Continental factories were already well established, did production begin in England. All but three of the English factories during the eighteenth century made only soft-paste porcelain.

The date usually assigned to the earliest productions of the factory at CHELSEA (London) is 1745. Charles Gouyn, goldsmith, and Nicholas Sprimont, silversmith, both of Huguenot descent, were the founders, backed by Sir Everard Fawkener, with the assistance, possibly, of the Duke of Cumberland. Gouyn retired early, so Sprimont's is the name mainly associated with Chelsea, and in 1758 he became the owner. The founders' training in metalwork is evident in the forms of Chelsea porcelain, and a reliance on silver shapes can be seen in the useful wares. Chelsea was also influenced by Chinese and Japanese porcelain and by the European porcelains of Meissen (plate 53) and, later, Sèvres.

Generally, Chelsea china is classified by its marks: the Triangle period 1745–49 (dates are approximate throughout), the Raised Anchor 1749–52, the Red Anchor 1752–58 and the Gold Anchor (Sprimont owner) 1758–70. Many Chelsea pieces, however, are unmarked.

Raised Anchor porcelain—the name refers to the embossed mark —is rare today. Among the figures are some fine models of birds (plate 54).

Colorplate 12.
About the middle of the eighteenth century, botanical painting became popular at some of the English factories. Much of the work, copied from books of scientific engravings, was extremely detailed. Two deep plates from the Chelsea factory. Decoration after Georg Dionysius Ehret, *Plantae Selectae* (1750). English, 1753–56. Diameter of each plate: 23.1 cm. (9⅛ in.). Marks: plate at left has Red Anchor mark, plate at right is unmarked. Cooper-Hewitt Museum, gift of Irwin Untermyer

53

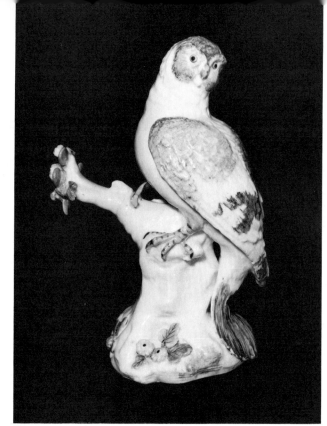

54

55

THE COCK & JEWEL.

THE VAIN JACK-DAW.

Students have long thought the Red Anchor the finest period of the factory and the high point of English porcelain making. Very fine soft-paste was made at this time. An accidental characteristic was the formation of transparent glassy spots in the paste, famous among collectors as "Chelsea moons" and plainly visible when a piece is held to the light. Botanical painting, copied from engravings of plants and flowers, was introduced (colorplate 12), and tureens and dishes were made in the shapes of animals and vegetables. The period is noted also for its superior figures, many copied from Meissen originals.

During the Gold Anchor period Chelsea began to take on aspects of the popular Sèvres style, with rich decoration, striking ground colors and much gilding. Also in the Gold Anchor period, figures were surrounded by *bocage*, a foliage background of tiny porcelain leaves, twigs and flowers, artfully constructed but rather fussy (plate 55). The factory excelled at toys, the most famous of which are the charming little scent bottles, three or four inches high, made in a variety of forms such as swans, hurdy-gurdy players, Chinamen and pineapples.

The Chelsea factory passed to William Duesbury of the Derby factory in 1770, and the subsequent porcelain is known as Chelsea-Derby (see below). The final closing of Chelsea came in 1784. About 1749–54 another porcelain factory existed in London, possibly a branch of Chelsea, whose history remains obscure. The factory's best-known piece is the figure of a girl in a swing, and its wares are called Girl in a Swing.

During the years 1744–76, soft-paste porcelain was made at Bow, in East London. Little is known of the first five years of the factory, and no wares can be dated from this period with any certainty. But in 1749, Thomas Frye, who owned a glass factory at Bow and was an engraver by profession, took out a patent for bone china, beginning a process that became world-famous.

Backed by London merchants, Frye at first called his factory New Canton, modeling many of his wares and their decoration on Japanese and Chinese porcelain. A few pieces survive carrying the name New Canton.

Bow has four periods identified by date: before 1749, 1749–55, 1755–60, after 1760. Products from the third period are, on the whole, the most valued. The painting of Bow figures is bright but delicate (plate 57), the tablewares are decorated with Oriental designs (plate 56), botanical painting or floral motifs (plate 58). Bow also made porcelain flowers (plate 59).

Bow was extremely productive, especially in tablewares, and some authorities say that it was the busiest porcelain factory in eighteenth-century England. Consequently, the collector has a wide choice among its porcelain. No regular mark was employed, but an

57.
Bow rooster figure, vividly painted in shades of red, on typical rococo base of the period. English, about 1755–60. Height: 10.3 cm. (4 in.). Unmarked. Cooper-Hewitt Museum, bequest of Mrs. John Innes Kane

58.
Among the many tablewares produced at the Bow factory, blue-and-white sauceboats with details picked out in gold are unusually fine. The form is derived from silver sauceboats. English, about 1750. Length of each sauceboat: 20.3 cm. (8 in.). Unmarked. Smithsonian Institution, National Museum of History and Technology, Sutherland Collection

anchor and dagger appear on some pieces after 1760. Bow was closed in 1776, when William Duesbury bought it and took its molds to his factory at Derby.

The DERBY factory, situated about forty miles south of Manchester, made a creamy soft-paste porcelain. The founder was André Planché, "chinamaker." His earliest products were made about 1750. William Duesbury, an outside decorator, the English equivalent of a *Hausmaler*, and John Heath became the proprietors in 1756. Heath went into bankruptcy in 1779, and Duesbury, who by then also owned both Chelsea and Bow, became sole owner of Derby.

The factory in its early days concentrated on figures (plate 60). Meissen originals were unhesitatingly copied and decorated in rather pale colors. Collectors watch for three or four patch marks (discolorations) underneath Derby figures, caused by the clay props

57

58

59

60

59.
Porcelain vases of porcelain flowers were nearly as popular in England as on the Continent. Bow flowerpot and bouquet. English, about 1760. Height: 17.8 cm. (7 in.). Unmarked. Smithsonian Institution, National Museum of History and Technology, gift of Mr. and Mrs. Richard Rodgers

60.
Derby Italian Comedy figures based on Meissen originals. English, about 1760–70. Height: 11.8 cm. (4⅝ in.) to 14 cm. (5½ in.). Unmarked. Smithsonian Institution, National Museum of History and Technology, Dr. Hans Syz Collection

61.
Chelsea-Derby figure of John Milton leaning on relief-decorated pedestal. English, about 1780. Height: 26.1 cm. (10¼ in.). Unmarked. Smithsonian Institution, National Museum of History and Technology, Sutherland Collection

that supported them in the kiln. "Patch family" is the common classification of these wares. Derby was marked in a variety of ways, most of them including a capital *D*.

After Duesbury acquired the Chelsea factory in 1770, CHELSEA-DERBY (or DERBY-CHELSEA) productions included not only tablewares but figures of notables such as Shakespeare, Milton (plate 61) and David Garrick. Some of these figures were colored; others were left unglazed, adopting the biscuit technique of French porcelain factories. French types of decoration, especially floral, were also used on the tablewares in the 1770s. Blue-and-white decoration in the chinoiserie manner continued to be made, however, as it was at other English factories. The marks of Chelsea and Derby were combined at this period.

The beginnings of the WORCESTER porcelain factory in the city of that name are credited to Dr. John Wall, a physician and amateur painter. Historians argue about the exact degree of Wall's involvement, but collectors long named Worcester porcelain of the years 1751–83 "Dr. Wall," and have made it one of the most widely collected English ceramics. (Oddly, 1783 is seven years after Wall's death.) Today the term "First Period" is preferred for Worcester made from 1751 to 1783.

Worcester was established in 1751 and proved successful from the start with its soft-paste, which, because it was made from a formula that included soapstone (steatite), differed from that of Chelsea, Bow and Derby. Worcester made many useful wares and appears to have specialized in sauceboats (plate 62), judging by the number of surviving examples. Jugs in many forms, candlesticks,

61

62

63

62.
Blue-and-white sauceboats, usually made in pairs, are a common form of Worcester. English, about 1751–60. Length of each sauceboat: 19.1 cm. (7½ in.). Unmarked. Smithsonian Institution, National Museum of History and Technology

63.
Worcester covered basket and stand with sprigged flowers. English, about 1770. Length: 22.9 cm. (9 in.). Unmarked. Smithsonian Institution, National Museum of History and Technology, gift of Mr. and Mrs. A. I. Sherr

flower holders, baskets (plate 63), leaf dishes and mugs were also made. Only a few figures came from eighteenth-century Worcester kilns, but despite their rarity they are of no particular interest. Worcester porcelain has the reputation of being exceptionally well made and free of crazing. Study of many specimens has convinced collectors that a characteristic of Worcester is a thin glaze that tends to shrink away from the foot.

Worcester's decoration is its main attraction. In the factory's early days, underglaze blue was used for chinoiseries, as were turquoise, citron, brick red and other brilliant overglaze enamels. Transfer-printed decoration (see Introduction) began quite early at both Bow and Worcester, and immediately became a major new process for porcelain decoration since it was easier and faster than hand-painted decoration. Robert Hancock, an engraver from Bow, introduced transfer printing (plates 64 and 65) to the Worcester factory, where he worked from 1757 and was briefly a partner (1772–74). Most of his prints are in overglaze black.

At Worcester transfer-printed decoration paled, literally, before the painting. A sumptuous palette was developed with extraordinary ground colors: apple green, mazarine blue, turquoise, lavender, claret and yellow. "Scale colors," so named because they were overlaid like fish scales, used as grounds were a Worcester specialty. The Worcester very dark scale blue is incomparable; scale pink, yellow and other colors exist but examples are rare. Reserved against these scale grounds, and framed in gold, were white panels in which flamboyant exotic

64

65

birds in varicolored plumage and equally exotic foliage were painted (plate 66).

Not all Worcester porcelain was painted at the factory; quite a bit was sent to London for outside decoration. Perhaps the most famous outside decorator painting for Worcester was Jeffrey Hamet O'Neale, who also did work for Chelsea and Wedgwood. His animals, illustrating scenes from Aesop's *Fables*, are especially well done.

Worcester was bought by Thomas Flight in 1783, and five years later King George III gave the factory permission to call itself The Royal China Works and use a crown in its mark. Worcester had many other marks, including the famous half-moon, pseudo-Chinese marks and the pseudo-Meissen crossed swords. Some pieces have merely a script *W*.

Between 1772 and 1814 Caughley in Shropshire, not far from Worcester, was the home of the CAUGHLEY porcelain factory, which used the soft-paste formula with soapstone in its composition. There was considerable production of useful wares decorated in blue-and-white, and the transfer-printing technique was also used (plate 67). In general the porcelain and its decoration resemble Worcester. The color of the Caughley paste by transmitted light, however, is usually characterized as yellowish in tone compared with the slightly greenish Worcester. The factory sold white china for decoration at other places. Caughley is famous for originating the familiar willow pattern, a pseudo-Chinese decoration endlessly copied by Staffordshire earthenware factories and still being produced. The marks were various and

64.
Transfer printing was a new form of decoration on porcelain introduced in England in the second half of the eighteenth century. Worcester mug with transfer-printed portrait of the King of Prussia (Frederick the Great, then England's ally) being crowned with a laurel wreath by Fame, and with panoply of arms. Black on white. English, 1757 (portrait is dated). Height: 8.8 cm. (3½ in.). Unmarked. Cooper-Hewitt Museum, gift of George B. and Georgiana L. McClellan

65.
Worcester teapot transfer-printed in purple with scene of classical ruins and figures in Turkish (?) costume. English, about 1770–80. Height: 14.7 cm (5¾ in.). Unmarked. Smithsonian Institution, National Museum of History and Technology, Alfred Duane Pell Collection

66.
Scale blue, one of Worcester's most famous colors, was often used on mugs and pitchers. The painting in the reserves of the pitcher shown here is of the type called Exotic Birds. English, about 1770. Height: 22.9 cm. (9 in.). Mark: pseudo-Chinese square mark in underglaze blue. Smithsonian Institution, National Museum of History and Technology, Sutherland Collection

67.
Transfer printing underglaze, as on this Caughley mustard pot and spoon, sometimes lent a rather fuzzy appearance to the decoration, in this case a Chinese garden scene. English, about 1780. Height: 9.6 cm. (3¾ in.). Mark: S (for Shropshire, the county in which Caughley was located) in underglaze blue. Smithsonian Institution, National Museum of History and Technology

C   S

included *C* or *S* (for Shropshire) and sometimes the half-moon taken from Worcester.

Porcelain was made for a few years at LONGTON HALL. Located in Staffordshire in what is now the famous pottery-making town of Stoke-on-Trent, Longton Hall was the only soft-paste porcelain factory in the area in the eighteenth century. Its history is even hazier than that of the other English eighteenth-century factories, but it seems to have operated about 1750–60, primarily as a manufactory for tablewares (plate 68). Production must have been large: when the factory closed in 1760 a sale was held of about ninety thousand pieces that remained on hand. A very strong blue, known as Littler's blue, after William Littler, one of the partners in the factory, is a distinctive color in the decoration of Longton Hall porcelain, and some pieces have been attributed to the factory on the basis of its use. Mugs, teapots and jugs were characteristic wares. Some figures, rather crudely modeled, were made. Most pieces of Longton Hall are unmarked, although a small number have crossed *L*'s, faintly reminiscent of the Sèvres mark.

The history of so-called LIVERPOOL porcelain is equally uncertain. The name Liverpool porcelain applies to the products of several eighteenth-century soft-paste factories, mostly very small, in and around the city of Liverpool. The problem of attribution is compli-

66

67

cated, and few wares can be ascribed to a specific establishment. Well-made soft-paste tablewares in blue-and-white were apparently turned out in quantity, and there were also flower-painted (plate 69) and transfer-printed pieces. Very little, if any, of the porcelain is marked.

At the LOWESTOFT factory, on the east coast of England, soft-paste porcelain was made about 1757–1800, mostly blue-and-white tablewares (plate 70) and occasionally figures. The factory specialized in mementos, small boxes, for example, inscribed with mottoes such as "A Trifle from Lowestoft." There was no standard mark. Because of an absurd error in the 1860 edition of William Chaffers's respected *Marks and Monograms*, it was long thought that China trade porcelain was either made or decorated in this little English town, giving rise to the name "Lowestoft" for all porcelain made in China for export. Needless to say, there is no connection between Lowestoft, which is soft-paste, and Oriental porcelain, which is hard-paste. Not quite dead even today although repeatedly refuted, the misnomer is perhaps the most famous blunder in ceramic history and a classic joke among collectors.

The three hard-paste factories operating in eighteenth-century England were PLYMOUTH, from 1768 to 1770, BRISTOL, 1770–81, and NEW HALL, about 1781–1835 (plate 71). The last is mainly a nine-

68.
Tureens in the form of fruits and vegetables have been made almost from the beginnings of European porcelain. The distinctive underglaze blue used on Longton Hall's cabbage tureen is called Littler's blue, after one of the factory's owners. English, about 1752. Height: 25.4 cm. (10 in.). Unmarked. Smithsonian Institution, National Museum of History and Technology

69.
Liverpool coffeepot and cover painted in red and blue. English, about 1765–75. Height: 27 cm. (10⅝ in.). Unmarked. Smithsonian Institution, National Museum of History and Technology, Sutherland Collection

68

69

70.
Blue-and-white feeding cup (used for children and invalids) from the Lowestoft factory. English, about 1775. Height: 9 cm. (3½ in.). Unmarked. Smithsonian Institution, National Museum of History and Technology, Sutherland Collection

71.
The harbor scene on this New Hall cup and saucer was painted by Fidèle Duvivier, a member of a family of china painters, originally from Belgium, who decorated for several English factories. English, about 1782–87. Height of cup: 6.4 cm. (2½ in.). Diameter of saucer: 13 cm. (5⅛ in.). Smithsonian Institution, National Museum of History and Technology, gift of Mrs. Judson Falknor

70

71

72   73

teenth-century factory and is included in Chapter 10. Plymouth and Bristol were more or less the same establishment, using kaolin found in Cornwall. William Cookworthy, a Quaker businessman, was the founder of Plymouth, moving it to Bristol in 1770.

Plymouth made tablewares (plate 72), both services and individual pieces such as sweetmeat dishes and open salts, and figures. The figures were often in sets like those of the Continental factories—the Four Seasons, for example. Plymouth has the reputation of having turned out a considerable number of flawed and discolored pieces.

Some forms of Bristol porcelain are rare. The factory's time was largely spent in making presentation services for such notables as Edmund Burke, but various tablewares (plate 73), figures (frequently in sets also) and hexagonal vases were made as well. Plymouth and Bristol were seldom marked. When used, Plymouth's mark was the chemical symbol for tin and Bristol's a cross.

Although English porcelain has always had a large following of collectors in England and the United States, it has never enjoyed the respect shown the great Continental porcelains. Rare examples sell for goodly sums, but the highest prices paid for English porcelain do not equal those for Meissen, Sèvres and Nymphenburg.

72.
Plymouth mug painted with scene of ruins in delicate overglaze colors. English, about 1768–70. Height: 15.6 cm. (6⅛ in.). Mark: chemical symbol for tin in red. Smithsonian Institution, National Museum of History and Technology, gift of Mr. and Mrs. Philip N. Israel

73.
Open salt, a relatively rare extant piece of this type from Bristol. Open salts were generally very elaborate in eighteenth-century English porcelain and often adorned with shells and other marine embellishments. English, about 1775–80. Height: 9.9 cm. (3⅞ in.). Unmarked. Smithsonian Institution, National Museum of History and Technology, gift of Eugene Buchanan

8 Later Far Eastern Wares

Throughout the eighteenth century, while factories from St. Petersburg to the English Midlands were turning out fine porcelain, Oriental wares in the Chinese taste continued to enter Europe, if anything in greater numbers. Having their own native porcelain in no way caused Europeans to lose interest in imports: one estimate has it that sixty million pieces of Chinese porcelain reached Europe in the course of the century. The demand for porcelain grew; the increasing popularity of tea and coffee alone insured standing orders for numerous vessels. And Chinese wares were much cheaper than European-made products.

The greatest eighteenth-century china collectors—Augustus the Strong, Madame de Pompadour, the Prince de Condé—continued to buy from the Far East regardless of the fact that they themselves had private porcelain factories. Even after Meissen had been in production to his satisfaction for several years, Augustus was still placing immense orders for Oriental porcelain for the Japanese Palace. He also bought up any Eastern porcelain already in Europe he could get his hands on. According to a famous story, Augustus traded an entire regiment of dragoons to the king of Prussia in return for a collection of 117 pieces of Chinese porcelain. Long dismissed as apocryphal, the story turned out to be true when original documents confirming the trade turned up in 1962.

During the eighteenth century, porcelain in China and Japan underwent many changes, and new types were sent to Europe, such as the K'ang-hsi blue-and-white, *famille verte* and *famille rose* porcelains discussed below. The Ming dynasty had been replaced by the Ch'ing (Manchu) in 1644, and the three eighteenth-century Ch'ing emperors, two of whose reigns were unusually long, gave their reign names to decorative arts made during their rule:

K'ang-hsi	1662–1722
Yung Cheng	1723–1735
Ch'ien-lung	1736–1795

Colorplate 13.
Chinese vase painted in red oxide and powder blue, depicting carp, a Chinese symbol for long life. Ch'ing dynasty, K'ang-hsi period (1662–1722). Height: 43.8 cm. (17¼ in.). Unmarked. Cooper-Hewitt Museum, collection of Stanley Siegel, gift of Stanley Siegel

The city of Ching-te-chen, for many centuries a flourishing center of China's porcelain industry, was now unrivaled as the world's center of porcelain making and astonished foreign visitors (still very few) with the countless smoking chimneys of its kilns. The Imperial Factory there thrived under capable directors, especially in the first half of the eighteenth century. Many records survive, documenting the operation of the factories during this period.

K'ang-hsi blue-and-white porcelain was avidly collected in Europe at the time and has retained considerable popularity in the West. The porcelain is pure white, the blue less vivid in tone. The style of the decoration is more pictorial and the drawing more carefully executed on the K'ang-hsi wares than on the blue-and-white wares of the Wan-li period (1573–1619) of the Ming dynasty which they somewhat resemble. Although the shapes of the porcelain were often made to Western models, the decoration on K'ang-hsi blue-and-white was largely Oriental in style.

Ch'ing porcelain has many other varieties, including strong background colors (colorplate 13). It was the age of *famille verte* and *famille rose* porcelain, so famous in the West. Used in their French forms even by those who are not French, the names are neither Chinese nor even eighteenth century. The division of Ch'ing enameled porcelain into families determined by their dominant colors was proposed by Albert Jacquemart in the 1860s. A French civil servant, he was a trained botanist accustomed to classifying species.

According to Jacquemart's scheme, porcelain whose decoration is primarily green translucent enamels is called *famille verte*. Other colors are used on these wares, and they are sometimes gilded, but green predominates. Other families are *famille noire*, with black (which is applied to the biscuit porcelain and overlaid with green) as the background color, and *famille jaune*, with a yellow background. *Famille rose* decoration, introduced about 1722–23, is dominated by an opaque pink enamel that has the interesting distinction of having come from Europe to China. The Chinese, beginning with Emperor Yung Cheng himself, became extremely fond of the color and put it fully to use (colorplate 15).

Having so ardently adopted *famille rose* decoration, the Chinese were in no hurry to let it go; in the middle of the nineteenth century they were still making porcelain in this style. These late objects were marked with the reign mark of Emperor K'ang-hsi, who had been dead for 150 years. Imitating earlier wares and marking them with earlier marks had long been a tradition in Chinese porcelain and was regarded as a gesture of respect toward the past.

Ch'ing potters did not desert monochrome decoration. Magnificent monochrome porcelains with superb crackle were made in many new colors, including brown, aubergine purple and lavender blue (colorplate 14). One color was a soft pink derived from copper red

Colorplate 14.
The art of crackle was perfected and exploited by Chinese porcelain makers. Vase with lavender blue crackled glaze. Ch'ing dynasty, K'ang-hsi period (1662–1722). Height: 41.6 cm. (16⅜ in.). Unmarked. Freer Gallery of Art

大清康
熙年製

大清乾
隆年製

known as peachbloom. The West loved it, and during the nineteenth century huge sums were regularly paid for fine examples. Peachbloom was used mainly on small objects since the glaze was difficult to achieve. A pale blue called clair de lune was also used on small, high quality porcelains.

Marks are of significance to the collector of K'ang-hsi porcelain. Hardly any T'ang and very few Sung examples have marks. With a few exceptions, the earliest pieces to show a reign mark were made in the Hsüan-te period (1426–35) of the Ming dynasty. Commendation marks were common on export pieces of the sixteenth century. Some Ch'ing porcelain for the home market is marked, but wares for export are virtually never marked. Marks are read from top to bottom, beginning at the right and working to the left. They may be stamped, incised before firing or painted in underglaze blue (rarely in any other color). Most Ch'ing marks are under the foot of the piece, usually enclosed in a frame. Hallmarks refer to a historic event or an honorary title. Only a few potters' marks appear, but marks of good wishes, good luck, congratulations, praise and dedication, and symbols like the peach (long life), were often used. Datemarks are important and were calculated on the basis of the Chinese cycle of sixty years. A single mark or a combination of marks may appear on a piece. Eighteenth-century factories constantly copied earlier marks as a compliment. Later the marks were deliberately forged, earlier wares being more desired by collectors and thus more valuable. Reference works give tables of marks to assist in reading those found on a piece. In spite of all this, it must be understood that many authorities play down the importance of marks and emphasize determination of date by quality and style.

Ch'ing porcelains named so far are porcelains in the Chinese taste, made for the home market, although a good many showed Western influence (colorplate 16) and, as has been said, a great many were exported to Europe. Other exports during this period included porcelains decorated only in underglaze blue which were sent to Europe for sale and painted there by European artists, mainly Dutch enamelers working in what they conceived as the Oriental style. "Clobbered wares" is the name given to this category. The name is not derogatory but derives from a shoemaking process said to be similar to the technique in which the enamels were applied.

Though a great deal of porcelain was specially made for export, as mentioned, in the late seventeenth century, the eighteenth century was the great export era. By 1700 the trade was so well established and so important to both Chinese and Europeans that special orders were accepted by the Chinese to make all sorts of objects (watchstands, for instance, or wigstands [colorplate 18]) whose use was alien and even unfathomable to the workers, and to decorate porcelain with signs and symbols (coats of arms, for example) that were unintel-

Colorplate 15.
The techniques of eighteenth-century Chinese polychrome decoration lent themselves to ever more elaborate painting, including narratives, as on this plate decorated in *famille rose*. Chinese, Ch'ing dynasty, mid-eighteenth century. Diameter: 25 cm. (9⅞ in.). Unmarked. Cooper-Hewitt Museum, bequest of Emily H. Chauncey

Colorplate 16.
Influences worked both ways between Eastern and Western cultures as a result of the China trade. The painting on this garlic-headed vase, which shows a seated female figure and two children amusing themselves in a garden, reveals an awareness of the techniques of Western painting, especially in perspective. Chinese, Ch'ing dynasty, early Ch'ien-lung period (1736–c. 1754). Height: 17.2 cm. (6¾ in.). Mark: four-character Ch'ien-lung reign mark in gray enamel on base. Freer Gallery of Art

COLORPLATE 15

COLORPLATE 16

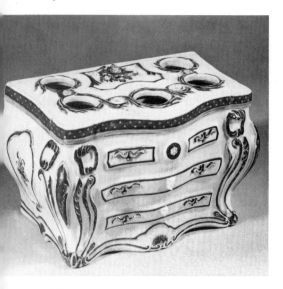

74.
Chinese export porcelain bulb pot made in the shape of a Louis XV commode, or chest of drawers. On the front are traces of the initials *AH* in gold. ("A.H." is unknown.) Chinese, about 1790. Height: 12.3 cm. (4⅞ in.). Unmarked. Cooper-Hewitt Museum, bequest of Mrs. John Innes Kane

75.
Garniture de cheminée, or mantel set consisting of two beakers and three vases. Chinese export porcelain made for an English family named Rigby and decorated with the Rigby arms. Chinese, 1750–60. Height of tallest vase: 29.2 cm. (11½ in.). Unmarked. Metropolitan Museum of Art, gift of the Winfield Foundation, 1951

ligible to them. This celebrated class of porcelain is called Chinese export porcelain, China trade porcelain or porcelain of the East India companies. It is of great significance in the history of taste and of major interest to collectors.

The customer in Europe or, later in the century, the United States had a wide choice: complete dinner services, often numbering hundreds of pieces, plates meant for display on walls or cabinets, jars, tureens, monteiths (colorplate 17), sconces, saltcellars, ladles, fruit baskets and so forth. The forms were often copied from European objects sent to China as models (plate 74). Trencher salts, for example, were copied from a late seventeenth-century European silver form. Most of the finished wares, however, were slightly Orientalized, inadvertently perhaps, but unmistakably, and this adds to their charm.

The porcelain body in which all these forms were executed was grayish-blue in color. The surface is often somewhat pitted, providing a texture described as "orange peel." Decoration was in the *famille verte* or *famille rose* palette or, most frequently, in blue-and-white. *Famille rose* was generally used for dinner services and other wares painted with armorial devices. Spanish and Portuguese noble families ordered these to their own design in the late seventeenth century, followed in the eighteenth by French, English (plate 75) and American families and organizations. Dutch, Danish, German, Swedish and

75

Colorplate 17.
A typical European piece produced in China for the export market was the monteith. Examples are extremely rare. Chinese, Ch'ing dynasty, K'ang-hsi period (1662–1722). Length: 49.7 cm. (19⅝ in.). Unmarked. Cooper-Hewitt Museum, bequest of Mrs. John Innes Kane

Colorplate 18.
Among items specially commissioned from the Chinese factories by Europeans were such curiosities as wigstands (also used as capstands) decorated in underglaze blue. Chinese, Ch'ing dynasty, eighteenth century. Height: 24 cm. (9½ in.). Unmarked. Cooper-Hewitt Museum, bequest of Richard Cranch Greenleaf, in memory of his mother, Adeline Emma Greenleaf

Colorplate 19.
The Great Seal of the United States with borders in underglaze blue on China trade mug for the American market. Chinese, Ch'ing dynasty, about 1800. Height: 15.3 cm. (6 in.). Unmarked. Smithsonian Institution, National Museum of History and Technology

76.
Chinese export porcelain sometimes depicted ships employed in the trade between China and the West, as in this cup and saucer showing the American ship *Helen*. The monogram is *EJ*. ("E.J." is unknown.) Chinese, about 1790. Height of cup: 6.7 cm. (2⅝ in.). Diameter of saucer: 14.4 cm. (5⅝ in.). Unmarked. Cooper-Hewitt Museum, gift of R. Thornton Wilson

other European armorial services are also known. While it is impossible to determine exactly how many were made, more than four thousand eighteenth-century services for the English market alone have been identified.

Export porcelain was generally made at Ching-te-chen and in the earlier days was decorated there. Around 1725 some of the enamel painting began to be done at the port of Canton, just before the porcelain was shipped to Europe. Two to three years would elapse between the time the order for porcelain was sent to China and the time the finished product arrived in Europe.

After 1784, when the new United States established direct trade with China, considerable amounts of Chinese export porcelain were made for the American market. There is no way of guessing how many pieces reached the United States during the height of the trade (1815–20), but one merchant in New York or Boston might receive a shipment from China of 15,000 to 20,000 pieces at a time, mostly tea services. The decoration of this porcelain included American ships (plate 76), American flags, American eagles, the arms or the Great Seal of the United States (colorplate 19), the arms of various individual states, the badge of the Order of the Cincinnati and (rarely) portraits of George Washington and other patriots. Famous services include one for Martha Washington that was so much admired it was reproduced in 1876 and in 1893 and again in recent years. China trade porcelain for the American market, while by no means as showy as some of the porcelain for the European market (the Portuguese is particularly colorful), is a perennial favorite with collectors.

Eighteenth- and early nineteenth-century export porcelain is usually considered by collectors to be the last Chinese porcelain of any consequence. Later wares whether for export or for home consumption consist mainly of imitations of earlier periods. Although Ching-te-chen was devastated during the T'ai P'ing Rebellion in 1853, when some of the kilns resumed operation they made fairly successful copies of Ming and Ch'ing porcelains, ordinarily with those dynasties' marks. Huge quantities of porcelain came out of China bound for the West all during the nineteenth century and into the twentieth, but after 1800 there were no notable innovations.

Japanese porcelain, taken to Europe by the Dutch in large amounts during the seventeenth century, shrank in importance during the eighteenth as Chinese export wares dominated the European market. Japan still made wares for export, particularly Imari, but most Japanese porcelain was now destined for sale at home. In both the eighteenth and the nineteenth century, most collectors believe, the quality of the porcelain declined.

After the seventeenth century, Korean porcelain was no longer exported to Europe. Western collectors, however, continue to seek out the earlier wares.

COLORPLATE 18

COLORPLATE 19

9   Porcelain in the 19th Century: The Continent

The tremendous political upheavals that began in Europe with the French Revolution of 1789 and continued for twenty-five years affected even porcelain production. During the Napoleonic Wars many factories were damaged or lost their staffs. The market for their wares was much restricted in troubled times. Among those that closed, never to reopen, were Frankenthal, Zurich, Cozzi, Chantilly and Buen Retiro.

Political and economic convulsions coincided with a marked change in taste. Beginning in the 1760s and 1770s and climaxing in the Age of Napoleon, Europe's arts were overtaken by a wave of admiration for and emulation of the "antique," a word applied to the whole culture, as then known, of the classical world of Greece and Rome. Everything from dresses to drawing-room carpets were styled in the antique mode, and there were Greek, Roman and Etruscan rooms in every fashionable house. The style, which remained popular well beyond the Napoleonic era, is now called neoclassical.

Porcelain styles were strongly affected by neoclassicism for about half a century. Among educated and well-to-do people it became fashionable to reject the old styles: one leader of taste sneered at the celebrated Meissen figures as "ridiculous dolls." Severity and simplicity of line were the aim of design, although this did not exclude superb painting and heavy gilding. Some of the most sumptuous porcelain of all time was produced around 1800. And busy designs, often inspired by Oriental models, continued to be made at many factories.

On the whole, however, today's collectors feel about neoclassical porcelains the way late eighteenth-century connoisseurs felt about early Meissen. Common words of criticism are "stiff" and "lifeless" and, perhaps most damaging of all, "technically good." This view has prevailed for some years, but nothing is more subject to change than taste in collecting, and already there are signs that these porcelains are regaining popularity.

Colorplate 20.
Throughout the nineteenth century the Russian factories produced some of Europe's most ornate porcelain. Cup and saucer from the factories of M. C. Kuznetsov. Russian, about 1900. Height of cup: 6.5 cm. (2½ in.). Diameter of saucer: 13 cm. (5⅛ in.). Mark: gold double-headed eagle and the name *Kuznetsov* in Cyrillic alphabet. Cooper-Hewitt Museum

Decorator painting a vase of neoclassical design at an early nineteenth-century European porcelain factory. Picture Collection, Cooper-Hewitt Museum Library

77.
Meissen dish with cover decorated in the neoclassical style with gilt palmettes, the centerpiece of a set with four supper trays (not shown). German, about 1810. Height with cover: 11.6 cm. (4½ in.). Diameter: 20.6 cm. (8¼ in.). Marks: crossed swords in underglaze blue and incised initials. Cooper-Hewitt Museum, bequest of Mrs. John Innes Kane

Porcelain in the neoclassical manner is not hard to identify: hollow vessels such as cups began to have straight sides (plate 78); handles were straight, too, and their bends rectangular instead of curved (plate 79); plates and dishes became flatter. Ancient forms, such as kraters and amphorae (handled Greek vases or jars), were often copied directly. In 1792, for instance, Vienna sent its master modeler, Anton Grassi, to Italy to find antique models for the factory to copy. Soon kraters and amphorae appeared on mantels all over Europe. Neoclassical pieces have a slightly heavy and solemn look; they can never be mistaken for the light forms of rococo porcelain. Porcelain objects became larger; more monumental vases were made. During the years of Napoleon's empire, productions, especially in France, were heroic in both size and decoration.

Flatter and straighter surfaces were an invitation to painters. A frequent criticism of neoclassical porcelain is that the porcelain became merely a surface for extended painting. Certainly painting did assume a new importance and often covered the entire object, hiding the porcelain body. The subjects were for the most part unimaginative: city views, landscapes, battle scenes, ancient ruins. Gold was used in abundance.

Neoclassical inspiration ran out about 1830, and from then until the end of the century historicism, also called revivalism, held sway. During this period earlier styles were copied in porcelain as in the other decorative arts. Virtually all porcelain factories copied their own old pieces (see plate 83), and newer factories copied whatever models they could get. From the collector's point of view, the proliferation of copies made from their old models and molds by factories such as Meissen has thrown some confusion across the study of porcelain.

The birthplace of European porcelain, MEISSEN, experienced great difficulties during the Napoleonic era. Both Meissen and Dresden were occupied by the French Army. Beset by these disasters and facing a declining market, Meissen experimented with many styles, none of which really captivated customers. The neoclassical was taken up in a rather tepid way (plate 77), as was the practice of painting elaborate pictures on the porcelain, including illustrations of scenes from current novels such as Goethe's *Sorrows of Werther* and copies of the paintings of the Old Masters. Jeweled porcelain after Sèvres was tried and jasperware (a fine stoneware) after Josiah Wedgwood. Finally, though not until 1833, when Heinrich Gottlob Kühn became director, even this great factory began, like others, to repeat its old successes. In the nineteenth century Meissen made rococo porcelain figures in countless thousands. Prosperity returned to the factory. These nineteenth-century figures, although taken from old models, are not difficult for collectors to distinguish, despite attempts to pass them off as old. Their poorer workmanship and florid painting in modern colors (the green is particularly noticeable) place them at a far remove from the originals by Kändler and Kirchner.

Meissen continued to make tablewares in *Zwiebelmuster*, or onion pattern, with underglaze blue decoration. One of the longest-lived of all porcelain patterns, having been introduced originally about 1735, it is still in production today at Meissen and other factories. The pattern was called "onion" because it was taken from a Chinese design of flowers, foliage and fruit that Europeans mistook for onions.

The VIENNA factory endorsed the neoclassical movement more enthusiastically than Meissen did (plate 78). The wares, inspired by neoclassical Sèvres, were well made, with much gilding and new ground colors: orange, brown and uranium black. The final burst of activity at Vienna before it closed in 1864 came in the Biedermeier period (characterized by a taste for the substantial), in which more painting and gilding than ever were employed.

At NYMPHENBURG during the nineteenth century some notable tablewares were made, and the famous Bustelli figures were cast again from the original molds, but in white. The FÜRSTENBERG factory also made neoclassical wares (plate 79) and reproduced earlier models. Both factories are in operation today.

The BERLIN factory was highly accomplished in neoclassical style. Silhouettes and cameolike antique heads were handsomely carried out with borders of ribbons. Berlin had the good fortune to have the continued support of the Prussian royal family, and many commissions came from them. High standards of painting, especially in local views and portraits (plate 80), were insisted upon. But the historicism of the era caught up with Berlin, too, and from the 1850s on porcelain in the old styles was made.

Among other German factories operating in the nineteenth century was a large group concentrated in the Thuringian section of what is now East Germany, where the natural resources were ample. The best and most collected Thuringian ware was produced at GOTHA (founded in 1757), which was active in the neoclassical style, with landscapes, silhouettes and medallions in its decoration (plate 81), and at KLOSTER-VEILSDORF (founded about 1760), which also produced neoclassical wares. Additional factories were established in Thuringia in the nineteenth and twentieth centuries. A number of these are still making porcelain, but few except Gotha and Kloster-Veilsdorf have attracted collectors. Thuringian wares are mostly rather grayish with a coarse texture and decoration described as "homey." Many of the Thuringian factories were inspired by Meissen to the point of forgery.

Kaolin was found near HOHENBERG, Bavaria, in the early nineteenth century, and the HUTSCHENREUTHER family started making hard-paste porcelain there in 1814. The firm was noted for its careful painting. Branches of this business were established later in the nineteenth century, and the firm is large and active today. Also in Bavaria, at SELB, the ROSENTHAL family in 1880 opened a porcelain factory that

78.
Vienna cup and saucer with typical neo-classical form and decoration. Austrian, 1800–1810. Height of cup: 6.6 cm. (2½ in.). Diameter of saucer: 13.4 cm. (5¼ in.). Unmarked. Smithsonian Institution, National Museum of History and Technology, Dr. Hans Syz Collection

79

80

79.
Fürstenberg teapot in the neoclassical style, cylindrical in shape with strap handle. German, early nineteenth century. Height: 11.5 cm. (4½ in.). Mark: F. Cooper-Hewitt Museum, bequest of Erskine Hewitt

80.
Berlin cup and saucer commemorating the victory of the allied forces at Waterloo in 1815, with portraits of Marshal Blücher (left) and the Duke of Wellington encircled by laurel branches. German, about 1815. Height of cup: 9 cm. (3½ in.). Diameter of saucer: 13.5 cm. (5¼ in.). Marks: scepter in underglaze blue with overglaze and impressed numerals. Cooper-Hewitt Museum, bequest of Erskine Hewitt

is now the largest porcelain manufactory in Germany.

In Switzerland, the factory at NYON began operations about 1780 and continued into the early nineteenth century (plate 82).

Of all the great eighteenth-century factories none perhaps has survived and flourished as well as ROYAL COPENHAGEN. Like so many other porcelain factories in the first half of the nineteenth century, it went through a period of economic and artistic decline, although producing a few fine neoclassical wares. The best-selling midcentury products were biscuit figures and busts after the great Danish sculptor Bertel Thorvaldsen. Earlier models were frequently copied throughout the century (plate 83). The revival of Royal Copenhagen belongs to the twentieth century (see Chapter 11).

In Russian porcelain, the era that began with the end of the Napoleonic Wars was a time of expansion and splendor. In 1817 no fewer than forty-five porcelain factories were operating in Russia; by 1870 there were seventy. Afterward, the number of establishments gradually declined, largely through consolidation. St. Petersburg (IMPERIAL FACTORY) followed the Sèvres-Vienna neoclassical style of gilding and painting galore on sumptuous grounds. Among the more unusual colors used as grounds were malachite, chestnut and lapis lazuli. As might be expected, military scenes of the Russian victories during the Napoleonic Wars were valued subjects for painted decoration. Next to St. Petersburg in importance was the GARDNER factory at Gielsk, near Moscow. It made services for the imperial family painted with the arms and mottoes of the various Russian orders of knighthood, and, later in the century, tea services with red roses in white reserves that were exported all over the world. Gardner was

81

82

also acclaimed for its peasant figures (plate 84). In 1891 Gardner was absorbed by the giant KUZNETSOV pottery and porcelain combine. By the beginning of the twentieth century, the Kuznetsov factories (colorplate 20) had become responsible for about two-thirds of the entire Russian ceramics industry.

Central to the neoclassical style in porcelain was the SÈVRES factory. After the 1760s, hard-paste began to be made with kaolin discovered near the town of Limoges. Soft-paste was gradually phased out, and by the early nineteenth century Sèvres had ceased making it. The factory had the good fortune to come under the direction of a remarkable man, Alexandre Brongniart, in 1800, and four years later, when Napoleon decreed his empire, Sèvres became the imperial porcelain factory. During the empire the porcelain was first marked *M. Imp^ie de Sèvres* with a date sign; from 1810 to 1814 the mark was the Imperial Eagle. Napoleon never overlooked any art that could contribute to the glory of his reign and seems to have had a special affection for Sèvres, which he favored with lavish orders.

Brongniart spent more than forty years at Sèvres. He was a serious student of ceramic art and wrote *Traité des arts céramiques*, a famous and influential book on the subject. He abandoned the manufacture of soft-paste porcelain altogether in 1804 for the new, hard-paste ware. New colors were introduced, and painting reigned. Magnificent services were created in which the painted decoration ran to Egyptian motifs, battle scenes, classical portraits (plate 85), medallions. Vases became larger and larger. Such size and florid decoration has so far not appealed to twentieth-century taste. Even finer, more detailed painting is found on the porcelain plaques turned

81.
Pair of Gotha covered vases with yellow grounds with medallions containing ciphers, and on verso silhouettes of a man and a woman (unidentified). German, about 1785. Height of each: 36.8 cm. (14½ in.). Mark: *RG*, the *R* for Wilhelm von Rotberg, original proprietor of the Gotha factory. Smithsonian Institution, National Museum of History and Technology, Dr. Hans Syz Collection

82.
Pieces from a Swiss tea service decorated with scattered blue cornflowers. Nyon factory, Switzerland, about 1790–1800. Height of teapot: 14 cm. (5½ in.). Height of each teabowl: 4.5 cm. (1¾ in.). Diameter of each saucer: 13.4 cm. (5¼ in.). Mark: fish in underglaze blue. Smithsonian Institution, National Museum of History and Technology

83

83.
Like most of the great European porcelain factories, the Danish Royal Copenhagen copied its own earlier wares during the nineteenth century. *Europa and the Bull* was modeled in 1783 by Carl Luplau; this copy was made in the late nineteenth century. Height: 26.5 cm. (10½ in.). Marks: wavy mark in underglaze blue, crowned with overglaze mark *D v R 576*. Cooper-Hewitt Museum, gift of the Trustees of the Estate of James Hazen Hyde

84.
Characteristic Russian group of three inebriated peasants from the Gardner factory near Moscow. Russian, about 1890. Height: 25.5 cm. (10 in.). Marks: name of Gardner factory stamped in red Cyrillic letters and impressed Russian imperial double-headed eagle. Smithsonian Institution, National Museum of History and Technology

84

COLORPLATE 21

Colorplate 21.
Paris vase of the Napoleonic era showing the strong influence of motifs from classical antiquity. French, about 1810. Height: 31.8 cm. (12½ in.). Mark: *Nast a Paris.* Cooper-Hewitt Museum, bequest of Erskine Hewitt

Colorplate 22.
Plate by Haviland and Company, Limoges, France, decorated by Edward Lycett, New York, about 1880. Diameter: 24.5 cm. (9⅝ in.). Unmarked. Cooper-Hewitt Museum, gift of Mrs. C. R. Dumble

COLORPLATE 22

85.
Jug or ewer from a Sèvres tea service depicting ancient Greek philosophers, each of whom is named (in this case Téléphanus de Sycione). Height: 21.6 cm. (8½ in.). Marks: cipher of Louis Philippe underglaze and date of 1840. Smithsonian Institution, National Museum of History and Technology, Alfred Duane Pell Collection

86.
Sèvres urn with cover in light gray-violet with white *pâte-sur-pâte*. French, about 1878. Height: 30.5 cm. (12 in.). Marks: overglaze *Decoré à Sèvres* with cipher *BF* and number *85*. Smithsonian Institution, National Museum of History and Technology

out in large numbers at Sèvres onto which masterpieces of canvas painting were meticulously (too meticulously, critics say) copied. Paintings by the Old Masters were thus reproduced for setting in furniture or for framing. Nineteenth-century tastes favored the framed plaques, which could be used as wall decoration.

After midcentury Sèvres repeated past successes in the same fashion as Meissen and other factories. Soft-paste porcelain was reintroduced and earlier works were copied. The famous biscuit figures were made once again. Some new ideas, however, emerged from this copying, among them the making of porcelain in the style of Chinese *sang de boeuf* and celadon. About 1859 a new decorating technique was introduced called *pâte-sur-pâte* (the term is also used in English), that is, relief modeling and painting with semiliquid white porcelain paste. The decoration is applied to a colored ground that shows through the film of semiliquid paste, producing a gleaming effect (plate 86). The technique was taken up by Meissen and Berlin and spread to England, where it was brought to high development.

Forgers had long been attracted to Sèvres because of its beauty and price, and the nineteenth century was their heyday. Under Brongniart the factory sold off large stocks of white soft-paste, which was then decorated by the enterprising buyers, many from England, and passed off as the genuine factory-decorated product. Some lightly decorated Sèvres had its decoration removed with acid and a heavier

85

86

87

88

decoration substituted, bringing a higher price. That one establishment engaged in tampering with Sèvres in England employed more than forty decorators gives some idea of the scale of this industry. The counterfeit decoration of Sèvres often did not match the body as to date and mark. Some porcelain carrying a pre-1780 date, for example, is jeweled, although the technique was not actually used at the factory until sometime later. Outright fake Sèvres was made by Thomas Martin Randall at Madeley, England, in the 1820s. Imitations were also made at Hanley and Coalport, and at many places on the Continent, including Tournai in Belgium, Soiron in France and Herend in Hungary.

Paris had a whole constellation of hard-paste porcelain factories, each with a rich patron. Most of these began in the late eighteenth century; nearly all closed between 1820 and 1830. Although the wares generally bear the mark of the individual factory, the porcelain is commonly referred to simply as PARIS, often followed by the name of the factory, which is identified by location: RUE CLIGNANCOURT (plate 87), RUE DE LA ROQUETTE, RUE THIROUX, for example. Rue Thiroux was under the protection of Queen Marie Antoinette, who allowed the factory to use her initial as its mark (plate 88). It made the porcelain milk pans for her famous play dairy at the Petit Trianon. Paris porcelain is very elegant: the neoclassical decoration and especially the gilding were used to great effect (colorplate 21 and plate 89).

Other nineteenth-century French porcelain factories are of minor interest to collectors, with the exception of a few LIMOGES factories. There was a branch of Sèvres at Limoges from 1784, and during the

87.
Paris sauceboat in the early neoclassical style from the Rue Clignancourt factory. French, about 1775–85. Length: 23 cm. (9 in.). Mark: *LSX* surmounted by a crown in overglaze red, *LSX* being the monogram of Louis-Stanislas-Xavier, Comte de Provence (later King Louis XVIII), patron of the factory. Cooper-Hewitt Museum, gift of Mr. and Mrs. Maxime Hermanos

88.
Queen Marie Antoinette was patron of the Paris factory in the Rue Thiroux. Covered cup and saucer decorated with her monogram. French, about 1785. Overall height of cup: 8.8 cm. (3½ in.). Diameter of saucer: 8.4 cm. (3¼ in.). Mark: overglaze red *A* with two crosses above. Cooper-Hewitt Museum

nineteenth century various hard-paste manufactories opened in the city. David Haviland, a china dealer in New York City, started a factory at Limoges in 1846 to make porcelain to his order. The factory was extremely successful, working mainly for Americans (colorplate 22). In 1878 the factory was turning out six thousand plates a day. HAVILAND mainly produced useful wares decorated with flowers in rather delicate colors and in modified rococo forms. The Haviland wares ordinarily are marked with different versions of the family name and the name of Limoges in various combinations; marks changed frequently. Other American firms had plants in Limoges also (plate 90).

Italy contributed little in the nineteenth century of interest to porcelain collectors. There were factories at TREVISO (1795–1840) and VINOVO (1776–1820), the latter, working in the French taste, being the more important. DOCCIA expanded, making not only fine porcelain (plate 91) but pottery. Countless copies of eighteenth-century Capodimonte and Naples pieces were made by Doccia. Venice's LE NOVE factory operated—but not continuously—from 1752 to 1835, making a variety of wares including tea and coffee services.

89.
Paris ice-cream dish with lining and cover. French, about 1795. Overall height: 25.5 cm. (10 in.). Mark: *B Z* incised underglaze. Cooper-Hewitt Museum, bequest of Mrs. John Innes Kane

90.
T. H. Rees, a New York City china decorator with a factory in Limoges, France, was the manufacturer of this pitcher, which was probably decorated in America. Nineteenth century. Height: 25.5 cm. (10 in.). Marks: *Rees* impressed and *J. M. Shaw decorator & importer etc.* painted in black letters. Smithsonian Institution, National Museum of History and Technology

91.
Doccia cheese plate with pierced lattice rim and raised center section. Italian, early nineteenth century. Diameter: 27.7 cm. (10⅞ in.). Unmarked. Cooper-Hewitt Museum, bequest of Erskine Hewitt

90

91

10 Porcelain in the 19th Century: England, Ireland and America

English porcelain received a substantial push in the late eighteenth century as a result of British economic policies. The impetus came first from a fifty percent duty on imported porcelain imposed in 1772, designed principally to keep out French porcelain. More important was the act passed in 1794 prohibiting the importation of any porcelain whatsoever into England in order to keep out goods whose sale might benefit England's enemies. The English had to fall back on the wares they could make for themselves. Bone china, which was softer than hard-paste and easier to produce than soft-paste, now began to be made in large quantities.

Although the Bow, Chelsea and Derby factories had been making a type of bone china since the middle of the eighteenth century, the standard English bone china recipe used to this day is generally attributed to Josiah Spode II, who is credited with developing it at his factory in Stoke-on-Trent in about 1800. The SPODE factory made tablewares of all kinds in quantity (plate 92), pastille burners, dressing-table items and ornamental vases. The decoration is characteristically elaborate—and to many modern observers, excessively so—with extremely intricate and brightly colored designs and heavy gilding. Chinese export porcelain inspired much of the design and there were transfer-printed chinoiseries. Spode specialized in the Japan pattern, which was influenced by Japanese Imari porcelain, and appropriated many Sèvres decorations. Typical English landscapes and views, often surrounded by flowers and garlands, were also used. Spode china is distinguished by the brilliance of its ground colors, which include an extraordinary dark blue, reds and lavender. Obscured as it is by the dazzling decoration, Spode's body is skillfully designed and made.

The Spode factory was probably the first (in 1842) to make what was referred to as statuary porcelain, commonly called Parian ware. A special variety of biscuit porcelain, vitrified, transparent and

SPODE

Colorplate 23.
A design of the Imari type is used on this service of Worcester porcelain of the Barr, Flight & Barr period. English, about 1807–13. Some pieces were decorated during the years 1813–40, when the firm was Flight, Barr & Barr. Height of compote: 15.3 cm. (6 in.). Diameter of cake plate: 20.3 cm. (8 in.). Marks: incised or overglaze in puce marks of Flight, Barr & Barr with lion and unicorn and three plumes near bottom; several pieces not marked. Smithsonian Institution, National Museum of History and Technology, gift of Mrs. Harcourt Amory

easily molded, Parian gets its name from its supposed resemblance to Parian marble. It was mainly used to make small statues; one factory at Hanley turned out half a million statues a year during the 1860s. Mythological figures, children, cherubs and living notables were depicted. Parian ware was made not only at Spode but at other factories in England and on the Continent and in America as well. Pitchers, candlesticks, jewelry and dolls' heads were also made in Parian. Not many pieces are marked.

The Copeland family bought the Spode works in 1833, and the mark, many times changed, often used the names Spode and Copeland.

DERBY was bought in 1815 by Robert Bloor from the Duesbury family. Under the Bloor management, biscuit figures remained in production (plate 94). Derby brought out from storage its second-rate wares, which were in the white, and decorated them. Although the porcelain was old-fashioned soft-paste, the decoration was in the contemporary enamel style suitable for bone china. In addition, Bloor produced an undistinguished bone china with many imperfections, which was decorated in floridly painted and gilded Japan pattern. In 1877 a new business called the Crown Derby Porcelain Company was started. It was permitted to add the word "Royal" to its name in 1889, and is still in existence. Many earlier Derby designs were reproduced, including the figures.

92.
Part of a Spode bone china coffee and tea service. English, 1800–1830. Height of teapot: 12.7 cm. (5 in.). Unmarked. Metropolitan Museum of Art, gift of the Rev. W. P. Eigenbrodt, 1894

93

93.
Plate from Chamberlain's Worcester factory decorated in *famille rose* enamels with Chinese tobacco leaf design. English, about 1800. Diameter: 22.6 cm. (8⅞ in.). Unmarked. Smithsonian Institution, National Museum of History and Technology

94.
Derby white biscuit figure of Hannah More, writer and teacher, modeled by George Cocker. English, about 1825. Height: 17 cm. (6¾ in.). Unmarked. Cooper-Hewitt Museum, gift of Mrs. Henry B. du Pont

F.B.B.

94

A number of changes in ownership occurred at the WORCESTER factory following the death of the leading partner of the firm, Dr. John Wall, in 1776, and that of William Davis, who managed the factory, in 1783. These changes are worth listing since collectors refer to the wares by the owners' names. Thomas Flight bought the factory in 1783 for his two sons, Joseph and John. Martin Barr joined the factory in 1791, followed by members of his family. In the 1780s Robert Chamberlain, a former employee, had established another porcelain company in Worcester under his own name (plate 93). This was united with the main business in 1840, and the firm then became known as Chamberlain & Co. A dozen years later another name change was effected when the W. H. Kerr and R. W. Binns partnership was formed. Upon Kerr's retirement in 1862, Binns established a new company called the Worcester Royal Porcelain Company Ltd. The successive name changes were:

Flight & Barr	1792–1807
Barr, Flight & Barr	1807–1813
Flight, Barr & Barr	1813–1840
Chamberlain & Co.	1840–1852
Kerr & Binns	1852–1862
Worcester Royal Porcelain Company Ltd.	1862–
(commonly known as "Royal Worcester")	

Colorplate 24.
New Hall tea service of bone china decorated in royal blue with reserve prints of mothers and children after engravings by Adam Buck. Six of forty pieces shown. English, about 1815–25. Length of teapot: 25.5 cm. (10 in.). Diameter of cup: 6.7 cm. (2⅝ in.). Unmarked; pattern number *1277* printed on bases. Smithsonian Institution, National Museum of History and Technology, gift of Emily Manheim

Colorplate 25.
On the right, Worcester "Dr. Wall"-period scale-blue cup and saucer dating from about 1765–75. On the left, an expertly forged cup and saucer. The forged pieces, which may possibly have been made at the Samson factory in Paris, show a distinctly yellowish color when subjected to shortwave ultraviolet light as opposed to the white color of the true Worcester under the same light. Genuine pieces: Height of cup: 4.5 cm. (1¾ in.); diameter of saucer: 12.1 cm. (4¾ in.). Unmarked. Forged pieces: Height of cup: 5.1 cm. (2 in.); diameter of saucer: 12.7 cm. (5 in.). Mark: pseudo-Chinese square seal mark in underglaze blue. Smithsonian Institution, National Museum of History and Technology

These changes are reflected in the marks, which carry the owners' names or initials in many combinations.

Worcester porcelain, like so much English nineteenth-century ware, is exceedingly ornate, decorated with landscapes, portraits and armorial bearings. Decoration of the Imari type was used (colorplate 23), as was a style derived from the Satsuma pottery of Japan. Pierced wares and porcelain plaques twelve inches square or larger were made. To its already rich palette Worcester added new ground colors and even made jeweled porcelain in the Sèvres style.

In 1889 Worcester bought the nearby Grainger Pottery, which made soft-paste porcelain and bone china. One of the more curious specialties of the GRAINGER factory were figures in lacelike draperies. They were made by soaking real lace in liquid china slip. The lace burned away in the kiln, producing a filigreed porcelain.

A bone china factory was established at Coalport, Shropshire, about 1796 by John Rose, who had worked at the Caughley factory. Much of the COALPORT porcelain, known also as COALBROOKDALE, was sold in the white in London to outside decorators from all over England. Rose's descendants worked hard to make magnificent ground colors imitative of Sèvres. Excellent reproductions were made of Sèvres, Chelsea and Meissen, with the original marks copied. Some of these have, unfortunately, changed hands as the real thing.

The NEW HALL factory, founded in the eighteenth century, made earthenware, hard-paste porcelain and bone china, some very colorfully decorated (colorplate 24). Patterns included flowers and mock Chinese figures. Transfer-printed decoration was frequently employed, often that used at various other factories. Since a great deal of New Hall is unmarked, some confusion exists in the attribution of wares to the factory. Tea and dessert services are characteristic products.

Also colorful, like Worcester and New Hall services, are the bone china ROCKINGHAM services, produced between 1820 and 1842 at a factory on the estate of Earl Fitzwilliam, its patron, in Swinton, Yorkshire. The sight of a Rockingham dessert service on display can be almost blinding with its brilliant colors, intricate decoration and thick gilding. The Brameld family, who ran the factory, insisted on using the best materials, superior potting and ornate decoration. In addition to tablewares—the dessert services being especially famous—Rockingham made wall plaques and ornamental wares heavily decorated with sprigged flowers. Rockingham was marked with the name of the factory or the name of Brameld or both. Earl Fitzwilliam's armorial device, a griffin, was sometimes used.

The old tradition of the porcelain arcanists and painters who worked at several factories continued into the nineteenth century. William Billingsley, a famous painter of flowers, was associated with the Pinxton, Worcester, Coalport, Nantgarw and Swansea factories,

MINTON

95

95.

Pâte-sur-pâte porcelain plate by the Minton factory. Woman with lyre and two putti. On reverse inscribed *Tragic Muse* and signed *L. Solon*, for Marc-Louis Solon, one of the best-known workers in the *pâte-sur-pâte* technique. English, late nineteenth century. Diameter: 23.8 cm. (9⅜ in.). Mark: *Mintons* printed on a globe. Smithsonian Institution, National Museum of History and Technology, Alfred Duane Pell Collection

Colorplate 26.

Historicism shows in the design of a Minton pilgrim bottle, modeled after medieval originals in pottery, with brown ground and a white cameo figure of a woman and two cupids. English, about 1890. Height: 26.7 cm. (10½ in.). Marks: *Mintons*, in gold letters, and *LS*, the signature of Marc-Louis Solon. Smithsonian Institution, National Museum of History and Technology

Colorplate 27.

An American version of Irish Belleek porcelain is seen in this large decorated tray in the shape of a mollusk shell from the Ott & Brewer factory in Trenton, New Jersey. American, about 1890. Length: 39.4 cm. (15½ in.). Width: 36.8 cm. (14½ in.). Mark: *Belleek O & B Trenton*. Smithsonian Institution, National Museum of History and Technology

among others. An admirer of Sèvres, he established a factory at Pinxton, Derbyshire, in 1796, where he made soft-paste porcelain on the Sèvres model. PINXTON closed in 1812, but Billingsley then founded NANTGARW (1813). He moved to SWANSEA in 1814. Both these Welsh factories made soft-paste porcelain. Their products, quite translucent and rather simply decorated, are collected today mainly in Britain, and all of them are rare. Collectors have to be wary of the outright fakes, complete with the proper marks, which were made in France in the late nineteenth century to capitalize on the demand for examples.

At Stoke-on-Trent the great firm of MINTON, known for its earthenwares, also produced bone china in quantity after about 1825. Minton is especially important because it produced a reasonably priced product that brought porcelain tablewares within reach of many more families than before. Like so much English Victorian china, Minton porcelain was heavily decorated and gilded, Sèvres being the main inspiration (colorplate 26 and plate 95).

No discussion of Continental and English porcelain of the nineteenth century is complete without mention of the remarkable firm of EDMÉ SAMSON ET CIE. of Paris, whose fame rests entirely on its imitations. Founded in 1845 with the express purpose of making "Re-

COLORPLATE 26

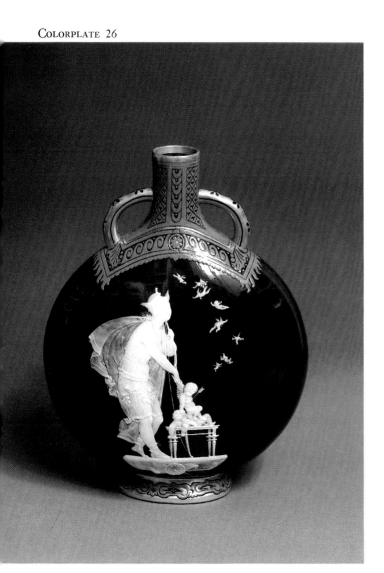

COLORPLATE 27

productions of Ancient Works Emanating from Museums and Private Collectors," Samson specialized in China trade porcelain, Meissen and Sèvres. Even soft-paste originals, such as the Sèvres, were reproduced, for the most part skillfully, in the hard-paste porcelain used at Samson.

Marks on some modern porcelain are the subject of much criticism and suspicion. Firms that today are still in the business of making "reproductions of ancient works" claim that all productions are marked with their factory mark, as well as the original factory's mark, Meissen's crossed swords, for example. Critics say that the modern mark is often omitted, leaving only a spurious original, and that some pieces have no mark at all. Thousands of such reproductions have undoubtedly been sold as eighteenth-century originals; many are difficult for even practiced eyes to recognize. Nowadays, however, short-wave ultraviolet light has proved helpful in the detection of forgeries (colorplate 25).

Quite off the beaten path in every way was the BELLEEK factory in County Fermanagh, in farthest Northern Ireland, where large deposits of feldspar and china clay were found in the 1850s. In 1857 porcelain and Parian began to be made at the factory, the Parian being used for some of the largest figures ever accomplished in the substance; a few were more than two feet high. But the factory's most famous product was the lustered Parian called simply Belleek (plates 96 and 97), which was greatly admired in the nineteenth century and is avidly collected in the twentieth.

Belleek is Parian with a white luster glaze that was unique to the factory at the time, although copied elsewhere later. The body is extremely thin, having been much manipulated, and very delicate in appearance. The glaze gives Belleek a sort of mother-of-pearl, or nacreous, look. Still, not everyone admires the effect; to some the glaze is "slimy." The combination of thinness and white glaze made Belleek especially suitable for marine subjects, such as dolphins, mer-

96.
Belleek bowl and stand. Irish, after 1891. Height of bowl: 7.2 cm. (2⅞ in.). Length of stand: 29.2 cm. (11½ in.). Mark on both: Irish wolfhound, tower and harp, and legend *Co. Fermanagh.* Cooper-Hewitt Museum

97.
Covered dish in the lustered Parian ware made at the Belleek factory in Northern Ireland. After 1891. Diameter: 21.8 cm. (8⅝ in.). Height: 9.7 cm. (3⅞ in.). Mark: Irish wolfhound, tower and harp. Cooper-Hewitt Museum

96

97

98.
Tucker & Hulme pitcher with floral decoration. American, 1828. Height: 24.2 cm. (9½ in.). Mark: *Tucker & Hulme, China Manufacturers, Philadelphia 1828*. Smithsonian Institution, National Museum of History and Technology

maids and sea horses. Intricate little openwork baskets were a specialty, hand-modeled by women whose fingermarks are still visible on the thin ware. Belleek was usually marked, commonly with a transfer-printed design of a tall round tower with an Irish harp on the right and an Irish wolfhound on the left and the name of the factory or the county in a ribbon. A slightly different version of Belleek was made in the United States at Trenton, New Jersey, by workmen originally from the Irish factory.

The United States is of course even farther removed from the old porcelain-making centers of Europe than is Northern Ireland, but a good deal of porcelain was made there during the nineteenth century. The motives for collecting this porcelain, however, have been mainly patriotic and nostalgic rather than aesthetic. An American manufactory of porcelain existed in the eighteenth century. BONNIN & MORRIS operated in Philadelphia in 1770–72. Examples of its porcelain are extremely rare. The earliest firm of which numerous examples are extant is that of William Ellis Tucker of Philadelphia (c. 1826–1838), which made bone china under the name TUCKER & HULME in 1828–29 and TUCKER & HEMPHILL in 1831–38. The decoration was neoclassical or floral (plate 98). American motifs, such as Gilbert Stuart's portrait of Washington, were employed, but examples are rare. One design showed Napoleon watching the burning of Moscow! Most Tucker pieces were unmarked, but some had the firm's name in red.

Parian ware was made in the 1850s at Bennington, Vermont, by the UNITED STATES POTTERY COMPANY, and in the 1860s at East Liverpool, Ohio, a pottery-making center. The UNION PORCELAIN WORKS operated in Brooklyn at the same time. OTT & BREWER in Trenton, New Jersey, from 1863 to 1893, called their works The Etruria Pottery, after Wedgwood's famous factory, and made Parian and Belleek from 1882 (colorplate 27). Also at Trenton, Walter Scott Lenox founded LENOX, INC., in 1896, making a soft-paste porcelain using the Belleek formula to which frit was added. Since then the Lenox formula has been modified. It became one of the largest and most important American porcelain companies and was commissioned to make china for the White House. In 1918 a dinner service of seventeen hundred pieces was ordered by President Wilson, and several later presidents have also ordered china from Lenox.

11 Modern Movements in Porcelain

The twentieth century began for porcelain about a dozen years before 1900. In the 1880s and 1890s new styles began to appear as a reaction against the endless succession of historical revivals and reproductions of earlier models. A new generation of modelers and designers at some of the oldest factories developed fresh techniques of manufacture and decoration. One of the earliest and most important of these innovators was Marc-Louis Solon, the famous maker of *pâte-sur-pâte* (see colorplate 26 and plates 95 and 99), a technique he was instrumental in introducing at Sèvres about 1859. Solon worked at Sèvres until 1870, then moved to Minton in England, where he remained for about thirty-five years. In the last decade collectors have become keenly interested in *pâte-sur-pâte* wares, which are on the market in sufficient numbers to encourage collection.

In the early years of the twentieth century, Art Nouveau, one of the new styles which emerged in Europe in the 1880s and 1890s, influenced porcelain design, although to a lesser extent than it did the design of earthenware. A few designers in the new style, like Hector Guimard (colorplate 28), worked in both kinds of ceramics.

The Scandinavian factories led in the use of new porcelain pastes, forms and decoration. Rörstrand, a venerable earthenware factory in Sweden, made some remarkable porcelain, strongly influenced by Oriental design (plate 100). The Royal Copenhagen factory experienced a strong revival, and is now one of the world's most respected porcelain factories. In the last years of the nineteenth century, under its famous art director Arnold Krog, who was to remain with the factory until his death in 1931, Royal Copenhagen introduced a new white porcelain. Very hard, it took underglaze decoration in soft, cool colors, such as blue. The modeling, especially of animals, was very fine. Also in Denmark, the Bing & Grøndahl factory, which had previously made stoneware, began to make porcelain and is still

Colorplate 28.
Hector Guimard, one of the most famous artists working in the Art Nouveau style, is best known, perhaps, as the designer of the Paris Métro stations. He did considerable work in the decorative arts, including porcelain. Glazed porcelain vase designed by Guimard and executed in Paris at the Sèvres factory. French, about 1908. Height: 27 cm. (10⅝ in.). Mark: impressed *Sèvres*. Cooper-Hewitt Museum, gift of Mme. Hector Guimard

99

100

99.
Jeweled salmon color *pâte-sur-pâte* plate in the Solon style, from the Berlin factory, dated 12 July 1890. Diameter: 35.6 cm. (14 in.). Marks: scepter in underglaze blue; orb over *KPM* in red overglaze. Smithsonian Institution, National Museum of History and Technology, Alfred Duane Pell Collection

100.
Rörstrand porcelain vase in the Chinese style with crystalline glaze. Swedish, 1904. Height: 15.4 cm. (6 in.). Mark: *KKL Rörstrand.* Cooper-Hewitt Museum, gift of J. Lionberger Davis

Colorplate 29.
Pair of porcelain bowls decorated in pastel colors from the factory of Richard-Ginori (formerly the Doccia factory). The twentieth-century wares of Ginori are outstanding in design. Italian, 1924. Diameter of each: 21.3 cm. (8⅜ in.). Mark: *Richard-Ginori 1924.* Cooper-Hewitt Museum

101.
Figure, one of a pair, of a woman with a child and fruit, in glazed porcelain by Kai Nielsen. From a group of figures entitled *Birth of Venus* by the Bing & Grøndahl factory, Copenhagen. Danish, 1913. Height: 23.3 cm. (9⅛ in.). Marks: incised *Kai Nielsen, 1913*; green-stamped underglaze trademark of three turrets over *B* and *G* and *KJØ Denmark* with *B* and *G* in underglaze blue. Cooper-Hewitt Museum, gift of Richard C. Greenleaf

doing so. Its well-potted wares, including both figures and tablewares, became and remain famous. A number of well-known designers, among them Kai Nielsen (plate 101), have modeled for the factory, and its annual Christmas plates, issued since 1895, are collected throughout the world.

At Sèvres designers such as Taxile Doat, Agathon Léonard (plate 102) and Théodore Deck, who became director of Sèvres in 1887, restored the factory's reputation, tarnished from having reproduced its own stock. New lines, including stoneware, were developed. During the 1920s and 1930s elegant dinnerwares in the Art Deco style were produced (colorplate 30).

Most of the historic German factories continued to reproduce old models until after World War I, when there was a period of rejuvenation. In 1919 Paul Scheurich, who had already worked at Berlin, Rosenthal and other factories, joined MEISSEN as modeler. He took many of his subjects from the eighteenth century—classical, Italian Comedy, Chinese—but simplified style and decoration. The colors, mainly mild, were unlike those of the eighteenth-century wares and included gray, brown, orange, light blue. Also at Meissen, Max Esser made animals and birds in streamlined contemporary style.

101

102   103

The factory reissued the Böttger stoneware of two centuries earlier, and continues to make tablewares, many in the older styles. The development of the NYMPHENBURG factory followed very much the same lines, with designers producing works in the Art Deco style (plate 103). All over the Continent the historic factories adapted their wares to the times (colorplate 29).

The English porcelain factories were slower to be affected by changing styles than the other European factories. For example, the DOULTON firm (which became ROYAL DOULTON in 1902), already in production as an earthenware factory at Lambeth in London, did not begin to make bone china at its works in Burslem, Staffordshire, until 1884. Most of its products were in the Victorian style (plate 104), but it must be added that Doulton also developed "art" stoneware, which was the name given in England to avant-garde design.

In the 1880s and 1890s able designers and painters created outstanding, if rather ornate, porcelain at the ROYAL WORCESTER factory

102.
Sèvres danseuse modeled in biscuit porcelain by Agathon Léonard. French, 1895–1900. Height: 42.2 cm. (16⅝ in.). Marks: stamped with the name *Sèvres*, the initials *AL* and the number 7/15, indicating that the figure is number seven of an edition limited to fifteen examples. Cooper-Hewitt Museum, gift of Mr. and Mrs. John W. Alexander

103.
Nymphenburg figure of America, holding reed flute, in white porcelain, attributed to Joseph Wackerle. German, about 1930. Height: 41.5 cm. (16⅜ in.). Mark: impressed escutcheon, lozenge. Cooper-Hewitt Museum, gift of the Trustees of the Estate of James Hazen Hyde

104.
Royal Doulton dinner plate decorated by C. Beresford Hopkins, signed on front. On back the word *Scotch*, identifying the breed of cattle shown. English, about 1902. Diameter: 25.5 cm. (10 in.). Marks: *Royal Doulton* in puce and impressed *6–66*. Smithsonian Institution, National Museum of History and Technology, Alfred Duane Pell Collection

(plate 105). The factory did many special order services for monarchs, nobles and statesmen, including some that ran, in eighteenth-century fashion, to many hundreds of pieces.

In the 1930s Dorothy Doughty, regarded as one of the most notable porcelain sculptors of the era, began her series of models of the birds of America for Royal Worcester. After the first series was completed in 1945, she began a second, which remained unfinished at her death in 1962. The birds, with their mounts of flowers and branches, were extremely elaborate and difficult to execute, requiring from twenty to fifty molds each. They were immediately successful with the collecting public, and gave great impetus to the manufacture of ornamental porcelain.

The Dorothy Doughty birds and other ornamental porcelains were produced in "limited editions" ranging from a few numbered examples to issues of literally thousands. Many English factories followed the lead of Royal Worcester in producing such limited editions for collectors. In the United States the late porcelain sculptor Edward Marshall Boehm, also noted for his birds, began issuing limited editions of his work in 1953.

Prices of these limited editions were high from the start, but the 1960s and 1970s saw a remarkable increase in price because of a growing worldwide interest in "collector's items" that included limited editions of commemorative wares of all sorts—plates, mugs, busts, vases. Spode, Minton and Doulton have been especially active in making commemorative porcelain items, most of them issued in limited editions.

At the same time other sorts of limited editions have been issued. Modern factories have been reproducing their older designs, though in a more scholarly and orderly manner than did their nineteenth- and early twentieth-century counterparts. For the most part these reproductions are plainly marked as such. Royal Copenhagen, for example, has reproduced its celebrated Flora Danica service, Royal Worcester has reissued its eighteenth-century Exotic Bird plates and Coalport has made new china based on its flower-encrusted Victorian models.

Chinese porcelain makers of the Ming dynasty copied Sung wares. Ch'ing dynasty porcelain reproduced outstanding Ming pieces. In Europe all the great factories—Meissen, Sèvres, Worcester and others—have at one time or another copied their own earlier works. While some of this copying was done for profit or from lack of new inspiration, much was done out of respect and admiration for the accomplishments of porcelain makers of the past. The tradition of making fine white translucent ware thus continues. And with it the collecting tradition. Fine porcelain, as much admired today as it ever has been, is studied, collected and cherished. From the Chinese connoisseurs of Sung porcelain of nearly a thousand years ago to today's collectors of eighteenth-century figures or contemporary limited editions is not really so far.

105.
Pair of Royal Worcester Near Eastern figures of a man and a woman, each carrying a jar, modeled by James Hadley. English, 1883. Height of man: 49.5 cm. (19½ in.); of woman: 53.3 cm. (21 in.). Marks: printed underglaze closed crown surmounting circle with four script *W*'s around crescent moon and number *51* in center, letter *U* below circle; also incised *Hadley 1883*. Cooper-Hewitt Museum, gift of Susan Dwight Bliss

12 Advice for Porcelain Collectors

Very few good collections of porcelain have been formed without considerable searching on the part of the collector. For many collectors the search for—and finding of—a desirable piece at the right price is, in fact, the chief attraction of collecting.

Getting acquainted with the principal dealers in porcelain and with the auction houses that sell porcelain—and nearly all auction houses have porcelain sales—is certainly the first step in collecting. There is no substitute for browsing among wares for sale. Studying auction catalogues and dealers' lists with prices is helpful, too, as is reading widely in books and journals.

Collectors are encouraged to use the resources available in museums to develop familiarity with major styles, factories and forms. Although museum examples may be unique, and beyond the hopes of the ordinary collector, many museums have on view a range of objects that can enable the collector to appreciate the breadth of collecting possibilities. Porcelain exhibitions are usually accompanied by instructive information about the objects, and certain museums have developed "study" collections which are invaluable to the beginning collector.

At some point one must get one's feet wet. A simple way to do this is to buy a few inexpensive pieces of porcelain made by a factory in which one is interested. Incomplete sets or pieces with minor defects or figures that are not of a rare variety would be good choices to begin with. They can be handled without trepidation and studied closely to learn how to judge the feel of the paste, the modeling, the shades of color in the decoration and the way in which the decoration was applied. Even though the examples are not of the highest quality, merely handling and observing them can be invaluable. Whenever a purchase is made, whether of study pieces or any other sort, the buyer should always obtain a complete invoice providing for each piece the name of

Colorplate 30.
One of a set of twelve Sèvres dessert plates in the Art Deco style designed by Jean Luce. French, about 1937. Diameter: 21.3 cm. (8⅜ in.). Marks: red overglaze shield with crossed L's and the word *France*. Cooper-Hewitt Museum, gift of James M. Osborn

the factory of origin and at least an approximate date of manufacture to act as a guarantee in the event further research casts doubt on the authenticity of any piece.

Study pieces are best examined in conjunction with books on the various factories and types of porcelain. The bibliography of porcelain is immense, and yet no book is complete. There is, for instance, no totally comprehensive book of marks. Constant use of the reference works on porcelain to learn about pieces one has already bought or perhaps is still considering is the only sure way to discover which volumes are the most helpful.

Every area and every factory in porcelain presents difficulties in attribution, in dating and in marks. Nothing is cut and dried about porcelain collecting. Discoveries occur quite frequently, and new information is published. At the same time, many areas remain relatively unstudied and offer unexplored ground for the collector. Porcelain collecting is a continually changing field, and a lively one, with its controversies over dates, factories, models and decoration.

Mention was made earlier of the use of shortwave ultraviolet light in the exposure of forgeries. These lights also reveal repairs that are undetectable by the unassisted eye. Many collectors today own their own hand-held lights; they are relatively inexpensive. Others use—for a fee—the conservation facilities of a local museum.

In comparison with what is required by many other collected objects, the care and preservation of a porcelain collection are relatively simple matters. Breakage is the only really serious danger; once porcelain is housed in a protected and not too warm place (to prevent cracking), it needs little attention. Dusting should be done with a camel's-hair or other delicate brush.

Glossary

arcanist, a craftsman who knew the formula, often kept secret in the early days, for making true porcelain.

biscuit or *bisque*, porcelain that has been fired once but not glazed.

blanc de chine, European name for fine Chinese porcelain with a milky white glaze popular in Europe from the seventeenth century on. It was much imitated at European porcelain factories, where the name was also used.

blue-and-white, decoration of Chinese porcelain with painting in cobalt blue under the glaze.

bocage, foliage decoration, which itself is made of porcelain, used as background to European porcelain figures of the eighteenth and nineteenth centuries.

body or *paste*, the mixture of clay and other ingredients out of which porcelain is made.

bone china, a translucent ware, neither hard-paste nor soft-paste porcelain, that contains kaolin, petuntse and bone ash.

botanical painting, decoration on porcelain, mainly eighteenth-century English, carefully delineating plants and flowers, for the most part copied from books of scientific engravings.

Callot figures, miniature porcelain figures, frequently grotesque, modeled after engravings from the work of the French artist Jacques Callot (1592–1635). Meissen, Vienna, Cozzi, Chelsea, Derby and other factories made Callot figures in the eighteenth century.

celadon, European name (originally French) given to Chinese stoneware and porcelain glazed in a color derived from iron oxide that varies from delicate green to gray-blue. Celadons were also made in Korea and Japan.

china clay, see *kaolin*.

china stone, see *petuntse*.

Chinese export porcelain, porcelain, mostly eighteenth century, made in China specifically for export. Also called *China trade porcelain* and *porcelain of the East India companies*.

chinoiserie, a European interpretation of what was believed to be characteristic of China, the Chinese and Chinese taste. During the eighteenth century chinoiserie was fashionable in all the decorative arts.

cipher, a monogram; intertwined initials.

crackle, glaze that has been crazed either accidentally or on purpose to produce a system of cracks. Highly developed in China, crackle decoration has been used by nineteenth- and twentieth-century Western potters.

crazing, the formation of a mesh of fine cracks over the surface of a glaze.

enamels, pigments mixed with finely ground glass used for overglaze decoration of porcelain. Enamels fuse onto the surface of the fired glaze at relatively low temperatures. Made from metallic oxides, they provide a wide range of colors.

famille rose, *verte*, *jaune* and *noire porcelain*, classification of Chinese enameled porcelain by the predominant background color of the decoration.

Fondporzellan, porcelain that has a colored background with white spaces reserved for decoration.

foot, raised support at the base of a piece of porcelain.

frit, the glassy compound of sand, alum, etc., which, when mixed with clay and water, is used in making some soft-paste porcelain.

garniture or *garniture de cheminée*, a porcelain set of three vases and two beakers, for mantelpiece decoration, made in China and later in Europe.

gilding, gold decoration applied to a piece of porcelain.

glaze, a glassy coating applied to porcelain by immersion or spraying. Glazes are produced in innumerable colors.

ground, background color.

harbor scene, a picture of shipping and quayside activity painted on porcelain; especially used by the Meissen factory.

hard-paste porcelain or *true porcelain*, porcelain made from china clay and china stone fired at a high temperature.

Hausmaler, an independent decorator who painted porcelain at home or in his own shop. The porcelain was obtained from the factory undecorated ("in the white").

Imari, originally the name of a Japanese porcelain made at Arita and exported through the port of Imari; later a term used to indicate heavy decoration in polychrome enamels on European porcelain similar to the Japanese product.

Italian Comedy figures, a series of comic figures derived from the Italian theater, which were produced at many Continental and English factories in the eighteenth century. Among the most famous of these commedia dell'arte figures were Colombina (Columbine), Arlecchino (Harlequin) and Pantalone (Pantaloon).

jeweled decoration, decoration of porcelain with drops of enamels applied in a dotlike fashion, giving a raised jewel-like appearance to the porcelain. Used at Sèvres in the 1780s and at Worcester in later years.

Kakiemon, a simple and delicate style of porcelain decoration characterized by asymmetry and large spaces left white. The name is taken from a dynasty of Japanese potters.

kaolin or *china clay*, a fine, white feldspathic clay essential to the production of hard-paste porcelain.

Parian or *Parian ware* (or *statuary porcelain*), a special kind of biscuit porcelain closely resembling marble, most often used for statuary.

paste, see *body*.

pâte-sur-pâte, relief and painted decoration using porcelain slip, a technique developed at the Sèvres factory about 1859 and later used in Germany and England.

petuntse or *china stone*, a feldspathic rock used in the production of hard-paste porcelain.

repairer, a workman in a porcelain factory who assembles pieces made from several molds.

reserve, a section on porcelain kept free of background color for painting or gilding or both.

sang de boeuf, copper-red glaze, Chinese in origin (Ch'ing dynasty), which has been copied by potters throughout the world. *Sang de boeuf* is French for *oxblood*.

scale ground or *scale pattern*, painted decoration overlaid to resemble fish scales especially associated with the Worcester factory of the eighteenth century. Blue was the most frequently used scale ground, but other colors are known.

Schwarzlot, black enamel decoration on German and Austrian porcelain of the eighteenth century.

slip, liquid clay used in the manufacture of porcelain objects or in their decoration.

soft-paste porcelain or *artificial porcelain*, porcelain made by mixing clay and water with the glassy compound known as *frit*. It is fired at a lower temperature than hard-paste porcelain.

sprigging, molded decoration applied as relief ornament to porcelain.

statuary porcelain, see *Parian*.

toys, a term used in the eighteenth century to describe various small objects such as scent bottles, toothpick cases and cane handles.

transfer-printed decoration, printed decoration on porcelain with a design taken from a copperplate engraving, applied by various processes.

Reading and Reference

General

BOGER, LOUISE ADE. *The Dictionary of World Pottery and Porcelain.* New York: Charles Scribner's Sons, 1977.

CHARLES, BERNARD H. *Pottery and Porcelain: A Dictionary of Terms.* New York: Hippocrene Books, 1974.

CHARLESTON, ROBERT J. *World Ceramics: An Illustrated History.* Secaucus, N.J.: Chartwell Books, 1976.

HILLIER, BEVIS. *Pottery and Porcelain, 1700–1914: England, Europe, and North America.* New York: Meredith Press, 1968.

SAVAGE, GEORGE. *Porcelain Through the Ages.* 2d ed. Baltimore: Penguin Books, 1963.

WEISS, GUSTAV. *The Book of Porcelain.* Translated by Janet Seligman. New York: Praeger Publishers, 1971.

Marks

CHAFFERS, WILLIAM. *Marks and Monograms on European and Oriental Pottery and Porcelain.* 15th rev. ed. New York: Dover Publications, 1966.

CUSHION, J. P., AND W. B. HONEY. *Handbook of Pottery and Porcelain Marks.* 3d ed., rev. London: Faber and Faber, 1965.

GODDEN, GEOFFREY A. *The Handbook of British Pottery and Porcelain Marks.* New York: Frederick A. Praeger, 1968.

Oriental

BEURDELEY, MICHEL. *Chinese Trade Porcelain.* Translated by Diana Imber. Rutland, Vt.: Charles E. Tuttle, 1963.

GARNER, SIR HARRY. *Oriental Blue and White.* New York: Praeger Publishers, 1971.

JENYNS, SOAME. *Japanese Porcelain.* New York: Frederick A. Praeger, 1965.

MEDLEY, MARGARET. *The Chinese Potter: A Practical History of Chinese Ceramics.* New York: Charles Scribner's Sons, 1976.

MUDGE, JEAN MCCLURE. *Chinese Export Porcelain for the American Trade, 1785–1835.* Newark, Del.: University of Delaware Press, 1962.

VALENSTEIN, SUZANNE G. *A Handbook of Chinese Ceramics.* New York: Metropolitan Museum of Art, 1975.

Continental

CHARLES, ROLLO. *Continental Porcelain of the Eighteenth Century.* Toronto: University of Toronto Press, 1964.

HONEY, W. B. *Dresden China: An Introduction to the Study of Meissen Porcelain.* New ed. New York: Pitman Publishing Corporation, 1954.

HONEY, W. B. *European Ceramic Art from the End of the Middle Ages to About 1815.* New York: D. Van Nostrand Co., 1949.

SAVAGE, GEORGE. *Eighteenth-Century German Porcelain.* New York: Macmillan Company, 1958.

SAVAGE, GEORGE. *Seventeenth- and Eighteenth-Century French Porcelain.* New York: Macmillan Company, 1961.

British

GODDEN, GEOFFREY A. *British Porcelain: An Illustrated Guide.* New York: Clarkson N. Potter, 1975.

GODDEN, GEOFFREY A. *An Illustrated Encyclopedia of British Pottery and Porcelain.* New York: Crown Publishers, 1966.

HUGHES, G. BERNARD. *Victorian Pottery and Porcelain.* London: Country Life, 1961.

SAVAGE, GEORGE. *Eighteenth-Century English Porcelain.* New ed. London: Spring Books, 1964.

Some Public Collections of Porcelain

UNITED STATES

Boston: Museum of Fine Arts
Chicago: The Art Institute of Chicago
Cleveland: Cleveland Museum of Art
Detroit: The Detroit Institute of Arts
New York City: Cooper-Hewitt Museum, the Smithsonian Institution's National
    Museum of Design
    The Metropolitan Museum of Art
Philadelphia: Philadelphia Museum of Art
San Francisco: M. H. de Young Museum (The Fine Arts Museums of San Francisco)
Washington, D.C.: Smithsonian Institution
    Freer Gallery of Art
    National Gallery of Art
    National Museum of History and Technology
Williamsburg, Va.: Colonial Williamsburg
Winterthur, Del.: The Henry Francis du Pont Winterthur Museum

ENGLAND

Cambridge: Fitzwilliam Museum
London: British Museum
    Victoria and Albert Museum
    Wallace Collection

THE CONTINENT

Amsterdam: Rijksmuseum
Copenhagen: Nationalmuseet
Hamburg: Museum für Kunst und Gewerbe
Leningrad: Hermitage
Munich: Bayerisches Nationalmuseum
Paris: Musée des Arts Décoratifs
    Musée du Louvre
Sèvres: Musée National de Céramique
Stockholm: Nationalmuseum
West Berlin: Kunstgewerbemuseum

Index

Acknowledgments

Cooper-Hewitt staff members have been responsible for the following contributions to the series: Concept, Lisa Taylor; administration, John Dobkin and Christian Rohlfing; coordination, Pamela Theodoredis. In addition valuable help has been provided by S. Dillon Ripley, Joseph Bonsignore, Susan Hamilton and Robert W. Mason of the Smithsonian Institution, as well as by the late Warren Lynch, Gloria Norris and Edward E. Fitzgerald of Book-of-the-Month Club, Inc.

The author wishes to thank the following for their kind assistance: Brenda Gilchrist, Lisa Little, Christian Rohlfing, Lisa Taylor and Joy Wolf of the Cooper-Hewitt Museum; J. Jefferson Miller II and Jennifer Oka of the National Museum of History and Technology; Hin-cheung Lovell of the Freer Gallery of Art; Arlene M. Palmer of the Winterthur Museum; Arthur Vitols of the Helga Photo Studio; and Joan Hoffman.

Credits

Cooper-Hewitt Museum, the Smithsonian Institution's National Museum of Design: All black-and-white and color photographs by Helga Photo Studio, Inc., New York, except Nos. 13, 15, 16, 50, 77, 87–89, 101 by George D. Cowdery

Robert C. Lautman: Color 19, 23–27

The Metropolitan Museum of Art, New York: 8, 10, 27, 30, 32, 33, 47, 51, 75, 92; color 6, 7, 11

Smithsonian Institution (National Museum of History and Technology): 20, 21, 24, 26 (Taylor & Dull), 28 (Helga Photo Studio), 29, 31, 35 (Taylor & Dull), 36, 43, 44 (Taylor & Dull), 53–56, 58–63, 65–73, 78, 81, 82, 84–86, 90, 93, 95, 98, 99, 104

Smithsonian Institution, Freer Gallery of Art, Washington, D.C.: 1–5, 7, 9; color 2, 3, 14, 16

LINE DRAWINGS: Fran Gazze Nimeck

Fig. 1.